George Buskin

More than forty Years in Gospel Harness

A Tale of Truth designed to Profit the Readers, young and old

George Buskin

More than forty Years in Gospel Harness
A Tale of Truth designed to Profit the Readers, young and old

ISBN/EAN: 9783337073374

Printed in Europe, USA, Canada, Australia, Japan

Cover: Foto ©ninafisch / pixelio.de

More available books at **www.hansebooks.com**

More Than Forty Years in Gospel Harness.

A Tale of Truth designed to profit the readers, Young and Old,

BY GEORGE BUSKIN.

-PUBLISHED BY

International Evangelical and Colportage Mission of Algoma and the Northwest.

1898.

INTRODUCTION.

"Let the words of my mouth, and the meditations of my heart be acceptable in Thy sight, O Lord, my Strength and my Redeemer." Psalm 19: 14.

In the words of David, this prayer is made at the commencement of this little narrative. The writer, like Amos, c n say, "I was no prophet, neither was I a prophet's son," yet methinks the Lord said unto me, "Prophesy (or proclaim) unto My people, Now, therefore, hear thou the word of the Lord" Amos 7: 14 16. But in that pathway too many times have I been like Jonah (chap. 1), and have fled from duty, and got into a sea of trouble; but by them have received instruction, finding, like many others, it is better to suffer for well doing, than for ill doing

It is written, "I believe, and therefore have I spoken." 2 Cor. 4: 1-3; Psalm 116: 10. This is every man's duty and privilege who owns God as his Father, Christ as his Saviour, the Holy Spirit as his teacher, and rejoices in the testimonies of Holy Scripture, as those who find great spoil, and in that path have found stubborn resistance from many a hard and unregenerate head and heart, but the Word of the Lord is the hammer that breaketh the rock in pieces, and must be used.

The believer is told to have no fellowship with the unfruitful works of darkness, but to reprove it, and that reproof comes best by walking in the light of God's countenance by His Spirit and His Word, making no league

INTRODUCTION.

with the inhabitants of the land, but overthrowing their altars, &c. Judges 2: 2, which in this day is the vain imaginations which exalteth itself against God's authority, whether in one's own heart or character, or in that of others, and as in the days recorded in Judges 5: 6. The highways of Israel were unoccupied, through the power of the enemy, and travellers waked through by-ways, which is illustrative of the crookedness of professed Christian character, in these days as well as in the days of Deborah's prophecy. The principles of righteousness are the same, whether under law or grace.

The power to do, endure, or suffer is of God. It is the overcoming faith which stands approved of God and man. God's side is always the overcoming side in the end. In Christ's address to the seven Churches in the Revelations, chaps. 2 and 3 each are approved or disapproved, by keeping His words and works to the end, which is to do well. In the various addresses it is an individual matter with all. To the Laodicean Church He says, "If any man hear My voice, and open the door, I will come in to him and sup with him." To the Philadelphian Church the word is, "Him that overcometh will I make a pillar in the temple of My God," and to those of Sardis He says, "Him that overcometh, the same shall be clothed in white raiment," and similar addresses to the others. Five of the Churches had gone wrong, but whether approved or disapproved as Churches, individual character was dealt with in each case.

Personal faith in God's sufficiency to keep, to care for, and to guide us apart from every circumstance and every creature, is the only acceptable path, saying and doing like Joshua, ' As for me and my house we will serve the Lord" If this is not the daily, hourly and continual prayer and purpose, in simple, childlike dependence and disposition, we are not in the condition we ought to be in. Christ Himself overcame and sat down on His Father's throne, and His character was that of a child, meek and lowly of heart. It was written of Him, " Unto us a child is born, unto us a Son is given." Isaiah 9. He is also called,

INTRODUCTION.

"The Holy Child Jesus." This is not merely a figurative expression, but positive character. "Led as a lamb to the slaughter." "The Lamb of God that taketh away the sin of the world,' and our pathway must be individually like unto His, or there is something wrong or wanting with us. Let us all continually pray that He would work in us that which is well pleasing in His sight, and faith with power, walking with Him as though there was no other to company with in earth or heaven; saying with David, "Whom have I in heaven but Thee, and there is none on earth I desire but Thee." Yet this implies fellowship with all who walk in the same path.

How wonderful and wonder working is the fellowship of saints. Think of Jonathan and his armour bearer, 1 Sam. 14: 1 23; David and Abishai, 1 Sam. 26: 6; Daniel and his companions, Dan. 2: 17, 18; Paul and Silas in jail, Acts 16: 25, 26 Then there is the solitary path and service of Noah, Abraham, Jacob and Joseph, Moses, David, Elijah, and of our Master, He "Who trod the wine press alone, and of the people there was none with Him." He looked on His right hand, but no one would know Him. He looked for comforters, and found none. But "through faith they subdued kingdoms, wrought righteousness, out of weakness were made strong, and all obtained a good report through faith, not having received the promise, but embraced them, and confessed they were strangers and pilgrims on the earth, looking for a city which hath foundations, whose builder and maker is God.' Heb. 11: 39. Let us then follow in the path our fathers have trod, and the blessing and honor will be ours as well as theirs, through the atoning merits of the sacrifice of our Lord and Saviour Jesus Christ upon the cross, of which Paul said, "God forbid that I should glory, save in the cross of our Lord Jesus Christ, by which I am crucified to the world and the world to me;' and so say all who are taught like Paul, and the writer with the rest; and the Holy Spirit has said, "Behold how good and pleasant it is for brethren to dwell together in unity." All taught of the Spirit will labour to exemplify it.

INTRODUCTION.

Having had a varied experience in Christian life and work, during more than 40 years, in the endeavour to make manifest my calling of God, who both sought and found His wandering sheep, far away from the Shepherd's fold, and have since then sought in various ways to constrain others to come to the same Saviour for life and blessing; and though oftimes blundering, being also weak and sometimes negligent, and have come far short of that I ought to have been, yet the record of some of the failures and fights, and the faithfulness and allsufficiency of our loving Father in heaven, who has never left or forsaken us of His mercy, and Who promises to lead all His people by the right way to a city of habitation, teaching us what we ought to be and what we ought to do, may serve by His blessing to strengthen some weak hands and confirm some feeble knees, and to constrain them to be strong and of a good courage in the grace of Jesus Christ, and to say aloud to the people, "Behold, your God shall come, and not keep silence," and not be unduly cast down by reason of the many tribulations, but to be possessed of Christ's overcoming faith, may continue faithful unto death, and receive the promised crown of life, which Christ will give to all who love Him; and if they cannot do better, than the writer at least, "go and do thou likewise."

GEORGE BUSKIN,

Of International Colportage Mission,
Toronto, Ont., 1898.

MORE THAN

40 Years in Gospel Harness.

An Apology for the Work and Worker of the International Colportage Mission of Algoma and the Northwest.

An apology for Christian work and for the existence of the International Colportage Mission, especially addressed in Christ's name to all objectors and to whom it may concern, with a short sketch of some of the missionary experiences and labors in Christ's cause in Great Britain, Canada, and the United States and on behalf of the mission.

It would be a somewhat strange proceeding for an ambassador representing legal authority to apologize for his deputed presence and commission to those to whom he may be sent. The fact of an apology, implies weakness, mistake, or misunderstanding somewhere; so also there positively needs no apology for pursuing Christian work, proclaiming or declaring the mandates of the King of kings, the Lord of heaven and earth, whether it be to princes, powers, or people of any land or nation, and all alike, both great and small, are God's servants whether they be evil or good, wise or simple, the message should be hearkened to and obeyed without delay; for we must give an account to God and be judged according to the deeds done in the body. There is but one standard for all. The word which Christ has spoken shall judge us all at the last day, herein accommodating the mistaken judgement of some and in encouraging the weak to trust in God and do the right. A criminal denying the authority of a magistrate and the law of the land to pass sentence upon him for his transgression against it, would be less unwise than a person to deny his obligation to God and His word, and that every sinner reconciled to God by the death of His Son, Jesus Christ.

is privileged to take upon him the ministry of God's word, is clearly established by one scripture passage alone, and there are scores of others. Jeremiah 23:28. "Let him that hath my word speak my word faithfully. What is the chaff to the wheat saith the Lord, is not my word like as a fire, saith the Lord, and like a hammer that breaketh the rock in pieces?" I have seen a light from a small match set miles of timber lands in flames which continued to burn for weeks and months. Such also is God's word, "which goeth forth out of his mouth. It shall accomplish that which He pleases and prosper in the thing whereunto He sent it. Again "ye may all prophesy" 1 Cor. 14:31-39. Brethren, covet to prophesy. So let us hold fast and use His faithful word. "What is the chaff to the wheat, saith the Lord." According to this scripture passage the prophecies of lies is the chaff of human deceit and invention which must be burnt up in the judgement, but the wheat must be gathered into the garner of the Lord—the wheat is necessary to nourish the children of God and men; so deal out whoever can. The Lord of heaven and earth has said, "He that withholdeth the wheat the people shall curse." Prov. The word of Christ is the bread of life, and like the five loaves and two fishes in Christ's hands which satisfied five thousand men, besides women and children and more left in the end than when they commenced to eat. Christ himself is the heavenly seed, the corn of wheat, which fell into the ground and died and brought forth much fruit to satisfy the hungry, longing starving souls of Adam's fallen race. He himself is the bread of life, of which if a man eat he will never die. We do well to remember that no leaven was to be put in the passover bread which typified Christ our passover, and with Him must be no puffy element of pride of personal possession or position and knowledge, or the like. Purge out the old leaven of malice and wickedness, saith the Apostle, that ye may be a new lump. This cannot be modified by codes or customs, catechisms, articles, counsels, conventions, synods, or corrupt interpretations. God's testimonies stand out fair as the moon and clear as the sun, and " the wayfaring man though a fool need not err therein," being the voice of our Father, God speaking in the ear of His servants, saying, This is the way, walk ye in it, obey and find blessing; refuse and rebel and the end thereof is death and banishment from the kingdom and glory of our Lord Jesus Christ.

To add to or to take from His word, is but a proud usurpation, robbing God of His authority and honor, and man of his privilege and blessing, and siding with the devil to circumvent the harmony of the kingdom of Christ, contaminating, the pure, and misleading the weak and simple. Christ said, Let him that hath ears to hear, hear, what the Spirit saith unto the churches, implying, hear God's voice in the scripture, rendering practical subjection thereto. He assures us that His yoke is easy and His burden is light, and His service a perfect law of liberty.

Paul says, "If we or an angel from heaven preach any other gospel than that which is preached, let him be accursed." Gal. 1:8-9. John says, "If they bring any other doctrine than that delivered, receive them not into the house nor bid them God speed," 2 John 10, the end of the commandment being love, out of a pure heart, out of good conscience and of faith unfeigned, which is ever the work of God's Holy Spirit. So the corrupters of God's grace tread a very dangerous path, sometimes selling their privilege for a mess of pottage, or like Ananias and Sapphira, keeping back part of the price, and sinning away the Holy Spirit, thinking to escape the judgement of God.

Let us stand in awe and sin not. Be sure your sins will find you out, is God's admonition, who has also given us strong consolation, and abundant assurance of our safety in Him. It is written, "They shall all be taught of God;" and again, "If any man will do his will he shall know of the doctrine whether it be of God." Christ is our counsellor. Man at his best is altogether vanity and of no account apart from Christ. God alone can satisfy the living soul. The spiritually dead have no knowledge of spiritual things; they are of the earth and speak of the earth. But the saint's conversation is in heaven from whence also we look for the Lord Jesus.

We read of Eldad and Medad prophesying in the camp of Israel, and some from envy wished them silenced. Numbers 11: 26. But Moses said, Would God that all the Lord's people were prophets, and that the Lord would put His Spirit upon them all. This doubtless was typical of the present dispensation in which the sons and daughters are to prophesy, by virtue of God's Spirit being poured upon all flesh. But many now like Joshua in his early days, and worse than he, envy and hinder their brethren's liberty, thinking their dignity is endangered, and that by a combine they can control their brethren to conform to their dictates, but Christ said, "Every plant that my heavenly Father hath not planted shall be rooted up." Luke 15:13. So let all consider whether or not they stand in God's counsels and in the fellowship of His Spirit, or in the wisdom and devices of men.

It has been my grievous experience to meet with some church officials and their families, whose conduct has not been in keeping with civilization, much less with that of the family of God, evidently priding themselves upon the abundance of their possessions, and the dignity of their official position, rather than having their hearts enlarged towards God and man by God's goodness and mercy to them and being humbled by a sense of their obligation to Him. This comes from having our hearts and minds taken from Christ and His word and placed on other things.

What was done in Hosea's day is being done extravagantly in this (see Chap 8:14.) "Israel hath forgotten his Maker, and buildeth temples." The gaudy structures and pleasant sounds therein have more attractions with the multitudes than loving and obedient fellowship with each other and with the Lord who redeemed us. These few general thoughts may serve to strengthen some believers in the liberty for service which is their heritage in union with Christ in any work in which the Spirit and Word of God may lead them, and if all sincerely pray,

"Guide me, Oh thou great Jehovah,
Pilgrim through this barren land."

We cannot but believe, that if we are willing to be led of Him He will guide us in His own right way for His name's sake, His spirit being a spirit of wisdom, power, love and of a sound mind. 2 Tim. 1:7. "Blessed is the man whose hope is in the Lord his God, who respecteth not the proud nor such as turn aside to lies." Psalm 40:4.

Sufficient has been said to show the perfect liberty and privilege every believer has to take part with God in His work. Acts 8:4, 11-20, shows that the disciples went everywhere preaching the word of God. Let us as individuals do the same and keep at it, and by the grace of God live out the testimony, being living epistles known and read of all men. The mosaic, priestly ritual is past and all fulfilled in Christ and all His people by Him, one and all, are made kings and priests unto God. Our High Priest having passed into the heavens, Jesus the Mediator of the new covenant, which God provided and not man, we are invited by Him to draw near unto God. (Heb. 10: 24), and we shall find delivering grace in each distressing hour. Let us do to each other the brother's part, remembering one is our Master, even Christ, and all ye are brethren. Do this and we shall be right; leave it undone and some day we shall find out to our grief we were wrong. God is no respecter of persons, but men are, to their everlasting disgrace and manifest folly.

This, then, so far apologizes for being occupied in Christian work, as an honest Christian we can do no other, while we are privileged of God to have His Word as a light in a dark place, to do other would be to turn back again and to multiply and make gods many and lords many, while some madly avow they are, but the disciple of Christ, can only conscientiously say. To us there is one God, the Father, and we in Him and one Lord Jesus Christ, and we by Him, 1 Cor. 8: 6, and any who would affect to be lords over God's heritage in word, in spirit, or act, are usurpers of an authority that they have no claim or title to, neither by their own wills, or by communities, companies, corporations, societies, or aught else, heaven's decrees remain unchanged to the end, though men may wander far astray, but in returning and rest shall ye be saved. The counsels of the Lord stand forever, the thoughts of His heart to all generations. Psalm 33: 1.12. Blessed is the people who know the joyful sound, they shall walk, O Lord, in the light of thy countenance, Psalm 89: 15, by thy favour shall they be exalted.

1854. In the month of Sept. 1854, the light of heaven in great mercy broke in upon my sin-blinded eyes in the preaching of God's word, the subject being, *The fire shall try every man's work of what sort it is*, 1 Cor. 3:13. It was in the old parish church of St Augustine's, Bristol, England. At this time I was altogether irreligious, and had avowed that there was no religion in me. It was the first time and last time I had entered the building, and it was there my parents were married, it being an old place, tradition says it was built to commemorate Augustine's preaching, near by, in the seventh century. This may be or may not be true. I entered it to note its antiquities, the city being renowned for its many antiquated buildings. The discourse awakened my interest, and I was convinced I was pursuing a wrong course, and reflecting upon the discourse while walking home, every word of which has long ago been forgotten except the Scripture text: "The fire shall try every man's work of what sort it is," I became increasingly conscious I was pursuing a wrong course, and concluded that if I did not turn quickly right about face and march, I might, like many others, young as myself, go over the precipice of time into eternity in a woeful manner, in the darkness, in an unprepared condition.

1855. I began to wish myself on safer ground, but feeling entangled in a net (it must have been the devil's) and from it I could see no easy or agreeable way of escape ; but during a half hour's walk home I had resolved to clear myself of everything and turn my back on all that was wrong and follow only the right. But I deferred it until the next 1st of January 1855. It was a secret between my soul and God. Get out of the net I would, but I knew not how, except abruptly to break from every companion and every evil habit. If I had at the time some social friend to have taken me by the hand I might at once have "ceased to do evil and began to learn to do well," but I had gradually slid into the enemy's ranks, and now to be a deserter and renegade from them would bring me abuse and derision, and for a time it was so, but death, certain and soon, was on the one side, and life eternal was on the other, and in God's great mercy early in the morning of January 1st, 1855, I said in my heart and soon made it manifest, that I had forsaken the army of transgressors. God's word says, "The way of transgressors is hard." They may call it by gay names, and bolster, wire and glue it up with bombast, defiance and deceit, but verily, its ways are hard and heartless, but Christ who cannot lie, says, "My yoke is easy and my burden is light," and I have never wearied of it. I was like Bunyan's pilgrim fleeing from the city of destruction. I knew but little, and had much to learn. What little I had known by kind and early instruction, had largely been marred, lost and buried, but the little I had left, I began with vigour to use, and the fruits of righteousness also began to enlarge.

Some over-wise people may, according to their custom, say this is but the work of the flesh. But God was in it of a truth, to move the flesh aright, and I can say in truth,

"Grace taught my wandering feet
To tread the heavenly road,
And new supplies each hour I need,
While pressing home to God."

I had resolved that all I knew to be wrong must go, and all that was right must be sought after. Among the first things I did was to get a diary, and reviewing the day, report myself in it. I soon gathered up all the helps I had to an ungodly life, placing them in the fire grate. I called my shop-mates to see them go up the chimney in smoke. Some wanted me to spare them and give them to others. I said they were no good to me and could not be to them. Then I was allowed three months to get back to the devil's way. But my purpose was firm and the terror of the Lord was upon me. Life lay to the right, and death in the wrong. The favour and blessing of God I resolved to seek and find. Three times on Sundays I attended service in the English church. The Sabbath soon had a charm for me that it never had before. The sun shone brighter, the birds sang sweeter, the church bells pealed with a charm unknown before, and the Sabbath was to me a day of sacred rest.

It was the time of the Russian war, when hosts of British soldiers left the shore, many of them to return no more. I know not how it was, but on Sunday morning I had read the account of the strife so long that I was too late to be in time for church service, as we had called it. The bells had stopped, and disappointed I looked across from the bedroom window to the spire, one of my good rules had fallen through, and I said, If I can't be there in time, I'll not go at all. So I began to inquire from myself what object I had in going there; and the best answer I could give, was, for prayer, I suppose. So, as I questioned with myself, I said, If it was for prayer I wanted to be there, I could pray at home as well as there. Then I concluded that I never had prayed, that I could remember, only when I was in danger of drowning, and on another occasion when I thought I had seriously hurt myself, then I cried that the Lord would spare me. I also found that I did not know how to make a prayer, and so I reasoned, If I wished to do right I must pray, for prayer was right; and if I knew not how to frame my words, I could bow my knees and take the attitude of prayer, and as I did so, there came into my heart the prodigal's prayer, "I have sinned and am not worthy to be called thy son." That was the beginning and end of my first voluntary prayer; and the answer I received in my heart was that the Lord did not despise me. How lovingly does the Lord invite us: "Return unto me, saith the Lord, for thou hast fallen by thy iniquities." It is our privilege to say like the prodigal, "I will arise and go to my Father, and will say unto Him, Father I have sinned and am not worthy to be called thy son." It was not long before I was started searching and reading the Holy Scriptures. A cousin had asked me if I knew how Satan came to Job. By this conversation I was led to read the book of Job, and was surprised at the instruction it contained and the beauty of its composition, and having read it through I started to read it through a second time, with increased pleasure and profit, then I said I have read many books, but have never read the Bible as I read other books. So I commenced at the beginning and read to the end, and the more I read it the more occasion and profit I found to do so, and in doing so it appeared to me that all other books I had read of merit, had got their principles and phraseology largely from it.

I put the Bible in my pocket, that I could read it at all times, and for many years accustomed myself to read nine chapters a day regularly—three chapters three times a day, besides other readings at intervals, so that I soon had a surface knowledge of nearly all sentences in the Scriptures. The Old Testament, and the gospels especially, were my delight, and the various Scriptures which I had learned in Sunday school came back very distinctly to my memory. For a long time they had been buried under the rubbish of ungodliness. I now began to take pleasure in ministering, as I was able, to the afflictions and necessities of others.

A shopmate and his wife, among them, were sick and both died and were buried together at the same time. I used to read the Scriptures to them as they lay sick, which was about Easter. The wife asked me one day after reading if I would pray for them and with them. I felt at the time unprepared to do so, for I had hardly begun prayer for myself, and a feeling of confusion came over me. I had two miles of a journey to their place, but it afforded me more joy and satisfaction than my former ungodly pleasures. I soon began on all hands, in a quiet way, to persuade my acquaintances to break off their sins by righteousness. Some opposed, some debated, some were persuaded, some, like Bunyan's Pliable, went a little way and then turned back, like the dog to his vomit, and the washed sow to wallowing in the mire. It is very grievous to think that many are called but few chosen, because they take pleasure in and love the wages of unrighteousness.

About this time I went to the services of a Dissenting congregation, not far from home, and where some of my acquaintances occasionally attended. I heard with profit expositions of Solomon's Song, and therefore the first time I witnessed the ordinance of the Lord's Supper, and was much impressed by it. I wished I were among the number of privileged ones. From a family friend I learned that they were Baptists, so that I would have to be baptized before they would receive me. This was a puzzle to me. I said I was christened in the Church of England, that my parents told me so. Was not that right? Our friend then gave me some counsel concerning immersion, which appeared altogether new to me, and I said I would look into the Scriptures concerning it. So I got the book of common prayer and the New Testament. I read the catechism, the baptism and the articles, and then I diligently searched the New Testament, and I took our Lord's example of what baptism should be. He was thirty years of age, and He went down into the water and was baptized and came straightway out of the water. That suited my simplicity, and in effect I said to myself,

"His way I see and I'll pursue,
Until in glory Him I view."

I wrote immediately to the minister whose discourses on Solomon's Song had so much delighted me, but in vain did I wait and seek an answer from him. How it was, I do not know, but I reckoned he was negligent. I hope he was not, but I felt so, and never went there again.

My parent's friend who had spoken to me was a member of the renowned Baptist Church meeting at Broadmead, Bristol, which was nearly a mile and a half distant from the former Baptist meeting house. As my letter had been unanswered she advised me to write to her minister, which I did, and at the first attendance there, I was more than ever stirred by a discourse from a stranger, concerning the man who found the treasure in the field. His whole discourse appeared to be directed to me, and I did not like being talked to in so public a manner. He appeared to know all about me, also concerning the letter I had written. I would have gone out if I could, but I was in the end of the front pew at the end of the gallery and close to the pulpit, and to go out would be to have all eyes on me. I was hot and restless and could not help myself. The man's discourse was good, but according to my mind, if it had not been so plain and strong I might have been better pleased with it, but doubtless it was the Lord speaking through the man (sometimes He does strange things in that way), although I thought there had been some kind of gossiping in which I had been reckoned up and now lectured. So when I got out I asked, Did you give the minister my letter? No! was the answer; Mr. Haycroft is out of town. I was more surprised than before. I soon received an interview. I was soon sized up and turned over, for instruction to one of the godly and instructed members who knew my condition better than I knew myself, who helped me to understand that "we are saved by grace, through faith, and that not of ourselves, it is the gift of God; not of works lest any man should boast; for we are His workmanship created anew in Christ Jesus unto good works which God hath before ordained that we should walk in." As this light shone in upon me, I perceived how little I understood about the atonement of our Lord Jesus Christ. It was like Egyptian darkness, such as I could feel. But blessed be God, I have been enabled to hold on to Christ who is the light and life of men, and better than all,. we are told that nothing can separate us from the love of God. which is in Christ Jesus. His strength is perfected in weakness.

When the brethren at Broadmead were satisfied that the grace of God was with me unto eternal life, upon the profession of my faith in Christ, I was baptized (or immersed) on November 1st, 1855, about sixteen months after my conviction of sin and then in danger of everlasting death.

1856. On the following 1st of January, 1856, at the New Year's day prayer service I could sing very happily :

"Jesus sought me when a stranger
Wandering from the fold of God ;
He to rescue me from danger
Interposed His precious blood."

During this time I had much joy in leading others to Christ. One was a fellow apprentice. He had no mother and his father was unable to work. He had capacity and energy, which outside of his work was largely directed to the theatre and profanity. I took him to my Baptist friend's house. He was washed and trimmed and dressed. Profanity and the theatre were forsaken, and he came under the influence of the gospel. Whether changed in heart I know not, but there was a great external change in him. He was killed by a fall a few years later.

Among the first Christian books I read after conversion was the Life of Samuel Budget, The Life and Journals of George Muller, Kieth on the Prophesies, and three volumes of John Wesley's Journals. Muller's Life and Work helped me to exercise faith in God, and Wesley's Journals stimulated my activity according to my ability.

For some time I held seven o'clock Sunday morning prayer-meetings at my Baptist friend's house, and in the evenings, after service, we would have singing of hymns. I did some work in Sunday school. I had an earnest desire to assist in the Lord's work in India or Africa. I made three applications. The answer to the first was, money was wanted, but not men ; they had plenty of men but no money. I then turned

(See page 11.) The Cathedral (Abbey) of St. Augustine. At a service held in the church opposite the Cathedral, Sept., 1856, commenced my repentance towards God which resulted in my conversion. I also took part in open air services held on green fronting the Cathedral, more than forty years ago.

to another point and was told to go to the Baptists with whom I met. After this I resolved that I would never ask of any man to undertake for me, but I would work for God and let Him work for me. Some said at this time that my conversion meant being a Baptist, but I said, I am baptized because it is right, and my purpose was to serve God; and my object has been to bring everything into that line. I have found the fellowship of saints to be happy, helpful and comforting, but the fellowship of profession is often as unreal as a ghost story, and there is nothing in it but thorns and nettles. The one is the divine life being manifested, and the other an artificial get up. To some 'tis pretty and pleasing, but there is no life. To look for life in it is but a disappointment. It is but dead machinery, a manufactured imitation of what things ought to be, but no life.

I pursued a sort of supernumerary church work as many do now, left to devise the way of action and to pay the cost, and largely to plod along alone. The Spirit of God doubtless moved me to action which for a time showed itself in admonishing, in a quiet way, all with whom I came in contact, to serve the Lord. I bought and distributed tracts and Bibles as far as my means would allow. I sought to break through the bondage which held in check my desire to further the grace of God. It was a new life to me and but little I knew, though the desire was fervent, there were grooves of religiousness the privilege of the few, but the fellowship of the Spirit, and faith in God to carry on the work for Him was altogether another matter, and the question is asked, How shall they do good who are accustomed to do evil? They must cease to do evil and learn to do well. There is God's school in which all are welcome, who will receive instruction, and it says, Whom shall he teach knowledge? The answer is, They that are weaned from the breasts and drawn from the paps, implying to be withdrawn from the rudiments of this world, whether they are religious or irreligious, for not all religiousness is godliness, but it is written, "As many as are led by the Spirit they are the sons of God." It is the same spirit that led Christ and all the prophets and apostles, and all the servants of God in all ages, which is a Spirit of truth, love, power, wisdom, and a sound mind, whatever any may say to the contrary, and implicit faith must be placed in the promises of God and this one among the rest, What man is he that feareth the Lord, him shall He teach in the way he shall choose. His soul shall dwell at ease and his seed shall inherit the earth.

The training of the head and that of the heart are two distinct things. Knowledge puffeth up, but charity or love edifieth. One is manufactured, the other divinely given. The knowledge that profiteth is the knowledge of Jesus Christ, whom to know is eternal life. This must come as the result of having the new heart and the right spirit. But some will say, This will not teach us grammar, music, geography, arithmetic, languages, science, and art. But the one who possesses the fountain must control the stream. Christ is the fountain of all these things. He made the heavens and the earth and all that in them is; therefore, to pretend to monopolize the stream and say the fountain does not control it, is madness, wickedness, and folly, and as soon as they learn to make the stream as free as the fountain, and the bombast of profession be renounced for simplicity and godly sincerity, the better. The monopoly of the streams of grace for schools and colleges, and communities, is an offshoot of Babylon whose sentence is to be destroyed. How can the oneness be in it for which Christ prayed: "That they all may be one as Thou, Father, art in me and I in Thee, that they all may believe that Thou hast sent me," when instead of having the spirit and character of father and brothers, we have that of lords, and brotherhood being largely, in name, only? None need be grieved by the statement, for we have a multitude upon whom the lordly title is lavished. Many others, not having the title think it becomes them to act as if they were privileged to pervert the character of Christ who said, "If I your Lord and Master have washed your feet ye ought also to wash one another's feet." This was no wordy pretence which some by cunning craftiness try to make it to be, but a positive act of loving service although He permitted and accepted the washing of His own feet with the woman's tears and to be wiped with the hair of her head.

1857. In 1857 there came to the Baptist Church a helper for the pastor, the pastor being somewhat a popular lecturer as well as preacher. He was employed as a city missionary in connection with the Church. He was a plain, practical, godly man, a little disposed to be inquisitive, but very kind. He soon laid hold of me, and as I was arranging to go to Australia, having an under current of purpose to serve God in doing so, though the business aspect was on the surface, this good man enquired of me my real motive in going to Australia. I acknowledged that business was the leading feature in so doing. So he said, My brother, had you said you were going there to serve the Lord, I would have said, Go, and the Lord be with you, but as you have said it is business I advise you to stay at home and serve the Lord. It is men the Lord wants and not money. The earth is His, and He can furnish all that is needed. I concluded his reasoning was right, and for a time we hitched on together for the work of the Lord. All my spare time was put in with him in street preaching, visiting and mission services. He broke me in for the first open air service. The first that I conducted in his absence, being directed by him so to do the subject was, Christ and the woman of Samaria. I tried hard in thinking it over to put it in an acceptable order but felt very much my inability, but when I had commenced I was quite at liberty, and what I had not seen before, they came from the far end of the street to hear, for what between timidity and determination, they heard a greater sound than they had been accustomed to hear, though my good brother was half as big again as myself. I found much profit and pleasure in his company for the short time I was with him. Something of his character may be judged by the following: Once when preaching in the horse fair, an Irishman threatened to strike him with a stick, to which he said, You must have my Master's permit first.

About the beginning of April I went to London. The nearest Baptist Church was Bloomsbury where the renowned and excellent preacher Wm. Brock was pastor. I had to be there early, as I took a seat on the side bench which I retained for more than 12 months though the meeting house was always overflowing.

From the commencement of my religious life I had an abhorence of rented pews. At Broadmead, Bristol, I was asked where I sat. I said, In the free seats, and they are very uncomfortable; to which the minister said, You should rent a sitting. I said, I have paid for two, but I prefer free seats.

I profited much by Mr. Brock's ministry; nis wholeheartedness, energy, ability, and candor served to rejoice my heart, and apparently all the rest. I felt the first morning that I was in the right place, and was well pleased to be present at every service. I have seen the building filled at 7 in the morning on the 1st Sunday in May, a service for young men and maidens.

On one occasion I invited a young man to the evening service who formerly attended my 7 o'clock Sunday morning prayer meeting in Bristol. He preferred worldly knowledge to that of Christ, and his deep conviction had passed away, and he now reasoned very skeptically. At this meeting his arguments were taken up and reasoned out satisfactorily to his face, and though he admitted his conviction of responsibility Godward, he failed to set his heart on God's ways and went from bad to worse. I had a pleasing evidence of the practical christianity found in the congregation. On a Saturday night a poor man asked if I could provide him a night's lodging. After a little talk I told him I would give him his lodging and breakfast if he would go to meeting with me in the morning. He complained of the unfitness of his clothes. Never mind your clothes, come with me, if you will. There were aristocratic folks present—Sir Morton Peto was a deacon. He was one of the firm who built the G. T. R. Road. Gen Havelock was also a member.—The poor man enjoyed the service. On coming out someone tapped him on the shoulder, and gave him a scrip of paper, on which it said, "Call at (address given) at 3 o'clock." He came back with a suit of clothes and a half crown. That's the kind of Christianity that tells; that couples good works with good words. "Cast thy bread upon the waters, and thou shalt find it after many days." I was privileged to have as a companion a godly young man of my trade as room mate. We had many a happy hour together. His name was Gideon Smith. He had earnestly desired to be in the ministry of the Congregational Church, but failed. I reckoned he had too much desire for elaborate exposition of scripture subjects, and not enough of the applied Christianity that goes about doing good; but he was an orderly, industrious, honest business man. Had he had money enough to have gone to college they might have turned him out a properly rounded machine-made minister; but as he had not, he did not fill the demand, and had to be laid aside. Education to-day too frequently goes as an equivalent for Christ, His Word and His Spirit. That is what the actions say, and those speak louder than words. Of course it is not becoming the times to say so, but it may serve as a drag to the wheels to stop going down hill too fast. That is the way the religious stage is going. But God still sitteth as the refiner and purifier of silver, And He shall purify the Sons of Levi and purge them as gold and silver.

In the fall of 1857 I went again to Bristol and had happy fellowship with my good friend and brother, the Missionary of Broadmead Baptist Church. His counsels and company were very profitable to me. I carried on a night school in the same little mission room the cost of which was largely met by a young man of the church, his father being a deacon. It was rather a poor and low neighborhood, and some of the attendants were turbulent, and put me to trouble and costs, yet there was a controlling providence.

One Sunday night while conducting service two young men were very annoying. A young woman of the company went for the police. I was asked if I would give them into custody. I said that all I wanted was to stop their uproar. The police took them out, and cautioned me not to admit them, as they would probably make it the occasion of robbing someone's house, but the next day we were relieved of them, one going with the Army and the other with the Navy.

There were four or more children of one family who attended the meeting, their ages ranging from 10 to 17.

Nearly ten years after this on a Saturday night as I was awaiting the connection of a train some miles from the city, a woman was also waiting in the same manner, and in a conversation I found that she was the mother of the children, and from inquiries I learned from her that her children were all doing well, so it may be that our labors, though feeble, have helped to keep aglow the sparks and fire of mercy, and grace.

1858. About this time I sought to pursue a pathway of faith in God, and Christain service, and at no time did I realize the Lord so near, was so overawed with a consciousness of His presence that His name was terrible to mention. But in pursuing the pathway I failed to endure the trial of destitution, so I went again to London, in the spring of 1858, but I soon found that my conscience accused me of unfaithfulness to my understanding, and I had nearly 12 months of intervals of darkness. When I got to London I was disappointed by not being able to find employment, and returning to the lodging with my friend Gideon Smith, after hunting several days for work, I came back on a Friday night dispirited, and said, "Gideon, you pray for me, for to-night I cannot pray for myself." Gideon did, and his prayer was heard; my trouble all vanished, though my circumstances were not changed. "Behold how good and pleasant it is for brethren to dwell together in unity," "Woe to him that is alone when he falleth, for he hath not another to help him up." Ecclesiastes 4:10. Therefore we should labor to retain fellowship with all in Christ and all who fear God.

On Saturday I rested, and prayed God to help and direct me. The same on Sunday with fasting, and on Monday morning at 7.20 I went to Westminister Abbey to make it manifest to myself that I committed my way to the Lord; and again at the 10 o'clock service. I then got my breakfast, wrote out the names of business men to call on, again returned to my lodging and asked the Lord to direct me as to how to begin seeking employment among the persons whose names I had entered down. I went into the chief place of business, praying which way to begin, to the right or to the left, and, while so doing a man came to me saying, "Have you a job? "No" said I, "But I do not know you." "I know," said he, "You were asking for work last week at our shop. Get on the bus and go to Hammersmith and inquire for—, they want a man immediately. So it was; I did not go to one of the persons whose names I had written; the Lord provided for me. Is any disturbed in the same way, let him take the same course. It was a very joyful time. While there I had pleasing Christian fellowship, but I soon returned to my old quarters, lodging, church and shop, my strength declined and I had to leave lodging and church.

I had very enjoyable intercourse with a company of young and old persons, who earnestly sought the Lord. One afterwards was for many years a missionary in Africa. On Sunday at first I met at 6.30 in the Methodist Church for prayer, ending about 9.30 in the Baptist Church, being at about ten various services during the day. If I do not enumerate them some may doubt it—prayer service Methodist Church 6.30; prayer with teachers at Baptist Sunday School between 9 and 9.30; school; morning church services; afternoon school; teachers' prayer service; young people's tea and prayer service; evening church service or ragged school; church or school prayer services; young people's prayer service. Young and old took part joyfully in these services. At the Baptist school there was an attendance of 600, in the ragged school an attendance of 1,000. In this school was a fife and drum band, and some of them the most poverty-stricken I have ever seen. One song was often sung with great glee:"Say brother, will you meet me on Canaan's happy shore?" I thought and purposed to start open-air services in Hyde Park with a band, but my physical weakness prevented me from attempting to carry it out. On Saturday night we had a prayer service, and Bible classes during the week, as well as church prayer services. We also did a little at open-air services. So my time was well filled up. I also endeavored to open a mission on the Surry side of Westminster bridge which was a poor and densely populated part, but was hindered; so I took a survey of Petticoat Lane and White Chapel, in view of opening a service, this being the Jews quarters for cheap wares, but never found opportunity, though many hundreds would be there on Sundays buying and selling.

In reviewing my experience with the Baptist minister's preaching at Lambeth, I found I profited much in the end by his ministry, as well as by Mr. Brock's, although the oratory and argument were lacking, for he dwelt continually on the atoning work of Jesus Christ, and that was what I much needed, so that I bless the Lord for his ministry as well as for Mr. Brock's.

During this time I was remarkably impressed and instructed to abide under the atonement of the Lord Jesus Christ. It was upon a fine summer's day, at noon, when I was in prayer in my lodging. I felt a deep consciousness of being before the Lord. I was afraid and trembled until I remembered that by the blood of Jesus Christ we must draw near to God. Immediately it sent a thrill of joy and peace, from the crown of my head to the souls of my feet.

In the shop I worked in I was frequently told of a man who had worked there many years and had died not long before. I have since heard that during his life he was known as Father Reeves. They told me he daily left his work and went into the timber yard, among the hardwood planks, to have prayer. He had been converted in the Westminster Road Methodist Church. When converted he could not read, but he set to work and learned to read his Bible, and his diligence and godliness was such that for many years he was leader of six classes in the church. His name was mentioned with reverence and respect by all his shop-mates. His death was occasioned by his being gored by a furious ox, on the street, which he had endeavored to hold in check by his umbrella.

During this time I was often very much agitated and grew very weak in body. I had a disagreeable companion to work with and frequently went for daily prayer to Westminster Abbey, after which my spirit was always calmed. On one occasion I was so driven that I had concluded to go and join the British Navy; but upon debating the matter with myself, I concluded it was better to bear the ills I had than to run the risk of getting into greater ones, from which I could not get away except by going overboard. The Lord mercifully delivered me from this besetment, and never since has the thought occurred to me to take such a course. Our Saviour

"Knows what sore temptations mean,
For He he has felt the same."

1859. In the spring of 1859, I left London and the good

providence of God directed my way to Brecon in South Wales, where for a season I had very joyful fellowship among the English Baptists, attending also the 7 o'clock Sunday morning prayer service among the Methodists. Finally I concluded to associate with a good active Christian brother in the town, who in days past had been occupied as a revival preacher and pastor in the Baptist church, but at this time, and for some years previous, had been preaching the Gospel through the country, sustaining a work among the poor, aged and infirm, both indoors and out. I was introduced to him on an occasion of his holding an open air service in the town and finally we hitched up together and worked heartily and earnestly for the Lord, sometimes beginning at 6 in the morning, and ending between 9 and 10 at night. It was a time of joy in the town; many young and old were gathered to the Lord. Prayer would commence at six in the morning and baptizings in the river at seven; meetings either for prayer or Bible reading every night in the week. The ice was broken in the river one morning to baptize an aged man, both walking home quite a distance in their wet clothes and taking no harm. It was here that I learned to break through some of the formalism that hindered work for Christ, and before doing so I reckoned the consequence, which meant opposition and persecution, and it was not long coming. My open air preaching was promised to be paid with brick-bats and pails of water and similar experiences; but I had a defender and helper in my good Brother and a kind-hearted romanish shopmate tried to disuade me by pitifully saying, George, I am very sorry for you that you should be so foolish, but the devil has lots of ways to deceive people if we listen to them. Bunyan says he put his fingers in his ears and went on his way, and that is an example for all to imitate.

One evening when holding open-air preaching and prayer upon the fair, we were invited by a woman to visit her husband who was very sick. When my good brother Prichard (for such was his name) saw him, he said, Dear me, you put me in mind of (forgetting now his name we will call him David Evans). Ah, said the sick man, I knew him very well. He and I were baptized together in the river. So my friend said, He is gone to heaven; I hope you are going there. To which he said mournfully, I don't know. Brother Prichard said, How is that? He answered, I have gone back. Drink and bad company have taken from me the light and joy of Christian life. We had prayer with him and we continued to visit him while life lasted, my last being at midnight, when he said, It is dark, it is very dark, but I am trusting in the Lord. In the morning his spirit had gone to God who gave it. We must every one give an account of our stewardship. The Apostle says, Take heed how ye hear. Drunkenness is often added to thirst, and men become like the company they keep. The Holy Spirit is grieved, the angel of the Lord departs, and the devil drives him, because he has not strength of himself to stand. The Lord says, "My spirit shall not always strive with man."

By the good will of acquaintances of my good brother, a meeting-house was designed and finally erected. I helped to dig out the foundation but it was not completed and opened till two years afterwards. The Lieutenant of the county gave the land. Things did not go as fast as I thought they should, and I resolved to go further.

1860. I had heard there was room for work on the island of Jamaca and there I resolved to go as soon as opportunity enabled me. I afterwards had a letter of commendation to some Baptist people there, leaving Brecon early in 1860, being commended to God by the prayers of the brethren and friends. I tarried a week in Merthyr with a Christian brother and then went to Swansea and began arranging for open-air work. I asked the co-operation of a Christian brother with whom I stayed for a few days, that together we might hold open-air services. He at first raised some objections, but I had the way made clear by enquiring from the police inspector if there would be any objections on their part. The only objection would be by having the thoroughfare blocked. So we arranged to hold the first of the meetings on Saturday night. The Welsh people generally were a religious and God-fearing people, old and young taking pleasure in searching the Scriptures, and not ashamed to carry a small family Bible under their arm when going to these meetings. At their funerals large companies of persons following would sing hymns with godly reverence through the streets as they followed the corpse to the grave. Numerous social cottage prayer services from house to house was the common custom of the people. Cheerful and kindly hospitality without grudging was almost as common as the day. So different to the affected courtesy of many professors which says to the caller, Will you come in? and at the same time hold the door and fill the little gap with their own figure, causing you to know that they would be more gratified with your departure than your company, showing very markedly the difference between Christian character and Christian profession, learning from custom and not from Christ, from the world and not from the word.

The Saturday night for the open-air service came round in due time, but at the last minute my friend refused to go; so I concluded that his negligence would not excuse my obedience, but it had been an effort to go single handed to hold such services, and I found it so at this time. When I came to the spot selected, the busiest portion of the town, large numbers of persons were there and a strong glare of gas lights. It must have been in January. As I looked on the crowd my courage failed me, thinking it too difficult to overtop their dealing and get their attention. Having had three places looked out in case there should be a failure, I thought I would go to No. 2. It was not quite so conspicuous, but when I got there the stand was occupied by a man blowing a flute. So I said to myself, Ashamed of Christ, then perhaps I may have to blow a flute like that poor man, for I possessed one. But as the ground was occupied I went to stand No. 3. When I got there that was occupied by a man singing songs. So I said again, Ashamed of Christ, I may have to sing a song like that poor man.

At one of the Baptist prayer services at Broadmead I had been deeply impressed with the singing of these words which I have never forgotten:

"Ashamed of Christ! my soul disdains
   The mean, ungenerous thought;
Shall I deny the Lord, who to man salvation brought?
   But should we in the evil day
From our professions fly,
   The Lord before the assembled world
The traitor will deny."

So I marched back to stand No. 1. It was unoccupied, and between purpose, fear and nervous excitement I gave such a roar that I felt like laughing to see the effect. I forget the subject of the address, but I had the attention of a big crowd for a considerable time, and on the Sunday morning I was present at the baptism in the sea—one who had been instructed from what I had spoken on the Saturday night.

I had arranged for work in the town, went to Bristol for a week, and on my return I commenced open-air services all around the town, and cottage prayer meetings, in one place which they told me was called, in English, Little Ireland. I may not give it correctly in Welsh, but its character will be better understood in English. It did not take long for me to be assailed with stones and dirt. While distributing tracts one of them said, "Get behind me, get behind me, we are a'fore you," meaning Romanism. On another occasion while holding a service there, being abused and surrounded, a little Irish woman with a shawl over her head, held them in check with a loud voice, saying, "Och, sure you're abusing the man and you know not what for; let us hear now what he has to say." Soon after a Welshman tapped me on the shoulder, saying, My friend, you are in bad and dangerous company here; come into my house.

For some time my tools had been delayed from arriving at Swansea and I had to return to Brecon concerning them. I had 17 miles of a walk between Merthyr and Brecon on a windy, rainy day, and at night I was hoarse and stiff with cold. My good and now deceased brother, S. Prichard, provided me a warm bath and pressed hard to be allowed to wash my feet, a custom in Wales, as is also the kiss of charity, but it was kindness with my friend, though custom is helpful in the right as well as opposed to the right when applied to the wrong. As the leopard cannot change his spots, neither can they do good who are accustomed to do evil. Jer. 13:23. My tools had left Brecon and were lodged at a wayside Inn in the hills between Brecon and Merthyr, so afterwards they came right to Swansea.

Some little time after this while holding open air preaching in the neighborhood of Little Ireland, I was taken in custody by the police and marched to the lock-up, a large concourse following on, many of my shop-mates being among the number. The Inspector said there was no need of bringing me there, and upon promise to appear before the magistrate in the morning, I was let go. I was not blocking any thoroughfare, for at this point one road branched into two. It was said to be the tavern-keeper who directed me to be apprehended. I was dismissed with a threatening of imprisonment or fine if I was brought there again. There were other towns besides Swansea, so I left on the following Monday for Bristol. Like Wesley, whose journals I had previously read, I reckoned that if I could not preach in one place I could go to another. In crossing the Bristol Channel in the boat, I still had opportunity of speaking for the Master. A Bible Christian said that baptism or adult immersion was right, and he would attend to it. After preaching I had a pleasing conversation with a Belgian Jew. He said, You Christians say there are three Gods; we Jews believe there is one God. So I gave him the Bible and asked him to read Isaiah 9:6: "For unto us a child is born, unto us a son is given, and the government shall be upon His shoulders and His name shall be called Wonderful, Counsellor, the Mighty God, the Everlasting Father, the Prince of Peace." I have never heard a man read the Scripture with the same external reverence. I met him again, but it appeared like the early dew, it had soon passed away—but I shall never forget the reverential character of his reading the sacred Scriptures.

I was now endeavoring to steer my way to the Island of Jamaica, and the friend who gave me a letter of commendation, also sent me to a Christian man of standing in Bristol who either then or some few months later said to me, If you wish to go to China your way is open now. There were two difficulties in the way, the language and the climate. My mind was set for Jamaica—although I do not know whether I made it a matter of much prayer.

From Bristol I went to Cheltenham. I made some Christian acquaintances there, attended the preaching of James Smith, a Baptist minister, several times, who wrote fifty little religious books published in an edition called the cottage library. I have sold many of them. One, called Light for Dark Days, was sold to a man when somewhat intoxicated. It passed from him to a second, then to a third person who was a young man, and soon after died being in the woods. Communication was not easy. When they saw he would die they spoke of getting a minister to visit him. He said they need not, he had got all he needed out of the little book, "Light for Dark Days." This was told me by one of the parties who has since died. We are workers together with God; one sows and another reaps.

In Cheltenham I continued holding open-air services. It was a period of much earnest Christian work. There were many earnest proclaimers of the Word in the highways as well as the meeting houses, among the rich and the poor. The Spirit of the Lord stirred many to activity, both in London and the provincial towns. Large and small social prayer meetings were being conducted in all directions. I did not tarry long in Cheltenham. I had no wish to stay long, for my purpose was to go across the ocean; but I was not allowed to stay long because I refused to join the trade clubs. This I did from principle. I had early in my Christian profession concluded that the Church of Christ in proper order should cover all necessities and extremities, and that other combinations to the Christian were unbecoming his profession, and though there is positively little faithfulness on the part of those who profess, sometimes from weakness, sometimes from ignorance, and sometimes from wilfulness, yet Christ and His Word remain the same. Faithful is their character. "If thou wilt return, O Israel, return unto me." Jer. 4:1. "Return unto me and I will return unto you, saith the Lord of Hosts." Mal. 3:7. I was not allowed to work at my trade because I would not join the trade club.

I then went to Worcester, found employment, but was unwell and unfit to work. There was a strike in the shop by the men. I was asked to leave—and by the employers to make a twelve months' engagement, neither of which I was willing to do. I yearned for Christian fellowship and was taken by the person I lodged with to a meeting of those known as brethren. I said my principles were close Baptist. They said they were believers and had also been baptized, and there were others among them that ought to be, and I might help them and they could receive me in the Lord if I could receive them, and so we did. I commenced holding cottage meetings. On Sunday mornings at 7 we met at the house of one of the brethren, and so from house to house. We had prayer services during the week, and open-air services through the town. When I was about to leave I was pressed to stay, and twenty persons from among them were baptized, twelve the first, and eight at a second time. After this I was taken into custody for preaching in the open air on Sunday night. I was alone. One of my helpers was unfit to be out, having had a heavy weight fall upon his foot. I had previous to this been annoyed by the unnecessary officiousness of a police, and received a thump on my back. My hat was jerked out of my hand, while a boy shouted, "Master, that man is a Roman Catholic." This night I was escorted to the station by the police. As I went I thought, Sunday night and all, if they are not ashamed, I am not. So putting on a strength of voice which made them more conspicuous than they wished, I continued the proclamation of the gospel to the steps of the station, when a woman from inside said with a loud voice, "The Saviour was led like a lamb, but this man is like a roaring lion." When inside I asked them pretty plainly if they were not ashamed of themselves to bring me there. One man said that they could not help it, as they had been directed to do it. So I said, Rather than do what my conscience told me was wrong I would beg my bread through the land. Soon after this two of my friends came and were responsible for my appearing before the magistrates the next day, if required, but I was not sent for.

Being in a weakly condition my mother wished me to return home. Having made the acquaintance of an invalid—belonging to Hereford, I was asked to visit there; so I took a journey to Brecon to see the brethren I had parted from some months before, and went to Hereford, held a cottage meeting and led an evening meeting at Bridgetown, returned to Bristol and then went by boat to Liverpool, intending to cross the sea for Jamaica as soon as possible. I was kindly received by brethren of the Disciple Church. I had somewhat of a tough time on the water, the sea was rough for a time. I enjoyed the sight of the mounting up of the waves, and the glorious power of the Creator who holdeth the waters in the hollow of His hand, but I became very seasick, and being very weak I felt it the more, till finally I fell upon the deck and was put to bed and was given a little of hot spirits and water, which made me sleep till we arrived in Liverpool some time on Sunday afternoon. I was very kindly received by brethren and I soon got to work in the gospel and the hand of the Lord was with me. The first day I went to work at my trade I made the acquaintance of a young open-hearted Irishman, whose heart the Lord had touched. I made a few enquiries of him and he told me that the governor was a pretty good man for a man of the world. I asked him if he was a man of the world, or not of the world; so he very candidly declared himself on the Lord's side. As I had not obtained a lodging my newly-found friend pressed me hard to lodge at the house where he lived. I did not like its appearance very well, but the dear fellow would take no refusal, so I went along, concluding the Lord was leading me. The result was, himself and his wife and his sister and brother-in-law all joined in Christian fellowship with the Disciple brethren. My second Sunday saw me preaching in the open air. My discourse was, Christ in the storm upon the sea. One of the brethren who led me to the spot had been a sailor. He afterwards said it was the best discourse I had given—it may have been in some measure from the experience that I had had a little before, although I had considered it before leaving Bristol.

On one of the Saturdays at pay time, my employer said to me, "Hamil says you are his brother; how does he make it out?" This was the shopmate previously referred to. So I had a little reasoning with him and he was very kind with me, but he said that though he had been a big teetotal talker (total abstinence) he always buttoned up his pockets when a man began to talk religion, because there was so much hypocrisy. Some time later he said to me, "The men tell me that you hold preaching services on St. George's Square, and that you get very excited." It is very common to call things by wrong games— mistaking earnestness and wholeheartedness for excitement and noise. Drawing a horizontal line, he said, "There is your level"; then putting another across it at about quarter pitch, in the fashion of boys at see-saw, he said, "What you go up on the one side of the line you have to go below on the other." This was his reasoning because of my sickness. I became too unwell to work but I did not know of any place where there was more opportunity for practical Christian work and a disposition to do it, than in Liverpool.

A little company joined with me in tract distributing, and house to house visiting, which was always preceded with prayer. I have always had a pleasant remembrance of the unfeigned and happy Christian fellowship that I experienced the few months that I was there. One of the brethren from Worcester came for a few days at Christmas. We had profitable Christian fellowship. On leaving he invited me, should I pass Worcester, to make a stay with him.

1861. Soon after New Year, 1861, I resolved to begin to make my way westward, tor Kingston, West Indies. I left the shop to go to Ireland, intending to tarry a while at Dublin and Cork, and then sail for New York, thence to Kingston. Calling to say farewell to some of the brethren, they pressed me not to leave, but to rest for a while. I returned to the same employer who made me promise to remain four months, which I intended to do, but soon after I was so weak that I could not endure the sulphur from the coke used in the smithy that I felt that I should have to go to the hospital if I continued, so I left for home.

Arriving at Worcester, the effect of travelling gave me symptoms of fainting of which I had several experiences during the year, in the workshop, meeting-house and in the home of my friends in Swansea, Bristol and Liverpool, and later in London, the effects of weakness and hard work.

At this time while in Malvern, ten miles from Worcester, I was directed to call upon a medical doctor there who also carried on a Christian work. His associates were all immersed believers. On calling, he received me very kindly, having previously heard of me. He invited me and my friend from Worcester to come to Malvern on the following Sunday, saying that he also had some Christian brethren coming over from Cheltenham, a distance by rail of about 35 miles.

While on the train between Worcester and Malvern, I gave an exhortation to those in the car about twenty or thirty persons, concerning the mercy of God in Christ, in which my friend joined; and on leaving, two men especially expressed their appreciation of what was spoken. My friend and I had a very enjoyable conversation as together we slowly made our way up the hill, a mile or two to the house of our brother, the medical doctor, where we were also greeted by the two men who had spoken kindly to us on leaving the train. At the little meeting which was conducted in a farm house in an orchard, fitted up by the good doctor as a house of prayer, there were gathered rich and poor, in homely, happy, unpretending fellowship. There was the wife of a Canon of the English Church, and the wife of a neighboring magistrate, and a Russian Count who lived not far away, who occasionally looked in.

The good doctor read and expounded Psalm 133, "Behold how good and pleasant it is for brethren to dwell together in unity," etc. taking us back to Genises 2, concerning Adam in Eden, "The Lord God made to grow out of the ground every tree that is pleasant to the sight and good for food," connecting with it the blessing and the never ending life. I also gave a word concerning Christ being declared to be the Son of God with power, by the resurrection from the dead. Rom. 1:4. Our fellowship was truly happy. The doctor being our big and elder brother, large of heart, and mind, and form, he entertained us joyfully and without grudging; not that any of us were actuated by anything but a Christian disposition.

Our Cheltenham brethren, on leaving, gave me a kind invitation to visit them, should I have opportunity. My friend from Worcester tarried till Monday and I was also pressed by the doctor to tarry, although it was my will to have returned to Clifton and Bristol, but the doctor used constraint. Malvern was a resort for invalids, and so was Clifton, but he told me very plainly that I may recover my health at Malvern, but I would probably die if I did not take advice and stay. He proposed my building some invalid carriages that would cover my costs while there. As I did not want to be unduly rash, I submitted my will to his, going to Bristol and returning to Malvern, and soon I had

"Taken in custody by the Police." (See page 27 and 29.)

to undergo a Hydropathic treatment, which meant getting out of bed at six in the morning and having a cold, wet sheet thrown over me, which necessitated me rubbing myself to my utmost, and also that of the attendant, and then to go for a walk of a mile or two up and down the hills before breakfast. This continued for some time, and the life that was in me was getting less and less, when I was obliged to conclude that such treatment may be very good for persons half dead with high living and idle life, but for one half dead with hard labor I concluded it would soon make an end of him; so I had to be obstinate, and say I could not stand any more of it.

Soon the good doctor went to Ireland and the meeting was left in my charge. I preached indoors and out, and had some evidences of God's Word prevailing both in Worcester and Malvern.

The bath attendant and I had occasion of walking together the same way. I briefly said to him, Do you take God's side in this world or Belial's, that is, the devil's? Oh, said he, I take God's side. I said to him, Christ's word says, If you do you are to be baptized. Some few days later we walked again the same way; so I said again to him, On which side are you now, God's or Satan's? On the Lord's, said he. I said I would arrange for his baptizing at once. He and his wife both confessed Christ in baptism. It was somewhat difficult work at North Malvern to baptize, but our friend, the doctor, had a zinc bath 7 feet by about 2½ feet, and it had to be filled by hand. My friend in Worcester also furnished himself with one, but his could be filled from the pipe of the water company.

After the doctor had left, I had a remarkable experience. I had baptized three persons from one house, the last being the wife of a laborer working upon a railway tunnel near by. He was an ungodly character and gave the people to understand that if his wife went to the morning service, at which the Lord's Supper was observed, he would upset the meeting. When the hour came the woman was there and so was the man, her husband. Different motives had induced them to attend, and when the good sister before spoken of, and others saw him up close to the little platform, they asked what was to be done. I did not know whether there was a constable in the neighborhood or not, so I said, Take no notice, but go on with the service just as though we did not see him. We had not sung much of the first hymn when he fell like a log to the floor. We all felt it to be a remarkable providential intervention, and like a dead man he was carried out into the orchard in which the meetinghouse stood, and we continued the service. He afterwards said that he would not attempt to molest us again.

About this time I was taken by one of the sisters a distance of several miles to see a woman who had had a remarkable vision. She lived in the valley, and the scenery all around was rich and grand,—the splendid timber, pasture hills and streams, with the fat sheep and cattle, reposing like David's picture in Psalm 23, the second verse. The woman was a widow about 40 years of age, living seemingly in rustic comfort and contentment, with a countenance very expressive of a godly disposition. After a few words of introduction the good sister said she had brought me to hear her relate the vision she had seen, and the circumstances relating to it. She said her heart was always affected when she had to relate it, and her tears flowed fast. She said her husband when in life was a source of much trouble to her, and she had resolved to drown herself and her child in one of the pools beneath the hills. She had arranged the time and place when her husband was asleep, but on the night she had resolved to do so her husband would not go to bed, so she could not leave the house without attracting his notice, so she lay down upon her bed and feigned to sleep, thinking to induce her husband to sleep. After a while she felt herself being carried from the bed, and was brought to a very high wall. A man on the top beckoned her up, and when she said she could not rise, his hand brought her up to the top, and there she saw a magnificent garden and a shining palace in the distance. She saw her grandmother and school mates, who had been long dead, walking there, and then she was taken by the angel to the palace, and saw the Lord upon a throne, and Jesus pleading for a sinner. The glory of the place was very great. Then said the angel, I must show you something more, and he took her down a darkened stairway, and came to a place where Satan and his imps were grinding sulphur to maintain the fires of hell. They tried hard to get hold of her, but the angel told her to keep close to him and she would be safe. She saw multitudes of people dancing, singing and fiddling, going on and into the lake of fire. She was then taken back to the spot at which she was raised to the top of the wall, and the angel said to her, You must now return to the world—seek to revelation, and you shall live in the first place, but if you live as you have been living, the latter place will be your home. At that she awoke, and all thought of destroying herself was forever gone;

her heart was changed, now she rejoiced in a Saviour's love. Some time after her husband died, and it was found that a tumor had grown in his inside which had caused his irritable disposition. I saw her but once, but I think I should know her after thousands of years have passed, her appearance and demeanor were so impressed upon me.

Finally I found I must remove from Malvern, and went to Hereford which was a distance of about 20 miles. Two little circumstances which occurred before leaving I will relate. In holding an open-air service I was pushed about by a hotel-keeper. My voice being strong, I suppose he thought it might not be acceptable to his customers,—but many of these men have no grief at the profane uproar of the godless drunkards, to whose fire of iniquity they add fuel. So reflecting upon his unwarrantable license, I went to him and told him that he must either apologize or I would take legal action against him. This served in some measure to bring him to his level.

About this time my friend from Worcester brought his workpeople to Malvern for a holiday trip, and while he and they capered about on the hills, I endeavored to drag my limbs after them, they bounding with strength which made my weakness feel the more painful. I thought, if they could feel my weakness they would move along more gently. Paul said, "Who is weak and I am not weak." It is a condition we need to cultivate more extensively.

Arriving at Hereford I commenced street preaching and house to house visiting, visiting also my friend who first invited me there who now had to have his diseased leg amputated. His friends could not exercise prayer in faith for his restoration. I was asked to conduct the morning service in a Baptist Church on two Sunday mornings. On the second occasion I had a strange experience. On the Saturday I felt too ill to work, so I sat down for some time to read. I often thought that my physical weakness gave me time to read and consider God's Word. While doing so there was a cry, someone was drowning. I ran out and jumped into a boat. It was a young woman on the opposite side of the river Wye, a beautiful stream. She was saved. I then felt all right and went to work. At night I bought some salmon—there had been a large catch that day near the house.

I went to bed purposing to rise early to get into the country for the morning service at the Baptist Chapel. In the morning when I awoke my mind was clear, but strength I had not. I was as a log with no power to move. My trouble was about the meeting. The friend who had gone with me the previous Sunday was not going, and he lived far away, and the only person in the house was an aged widow, my landlady. There I lay with no power to move. I prayed for strength to get out of bed. I had in my box a little port wine which I used in remembering the Lord's death. I took a little of it and had strength to dress. I resolved I would go as far as my strength would enable me, and if I fell, I then could go no farther. I attempted to go down stairs, but had to hold very tight to keep from falling to the bottom. I felt I must take something to eat, although I had no appetite, so my landlady boiled the salmon, and with some vinegar I ate a little. Then I wrote a few lines to my friend in Brecon, asking his prayers, for I knew, humanly speaking, my days were few.

I began my journey to tell the people I was too sick to conduct the service. I posted my letter to my friend, and had not gone far when a person with a spring cart met me to drive me out. As we went along, my bones were like the joints of a worn-out chair, rocking any and every way.

I had some pleasant talk with the young man who drove me, concerning his personal standing before God, when suddenly he lost his kindly manner and expression, and said, I suppose you will have a long account to give the people of what I have said to you. The Lord searches the heart, but the devil will always invent some objection to it, and by his lies try to frighten the weak and simple into delaying their escape from his bondage.

When I reached the meeting-house the people gathered around me enquiring concerning my health. I told them I had come out to tell them that I was too unwell to take the service, but as I felt a little better, if they would give out the hymns and lead the prayers I would conduct the reading and exhortation, which I did, in a very measured way. They were satisfied and I returned, feeling better than on the previous Sunday. So the Lord gives us strength according to our day.

"When united trials meet,
He shows a path of safe retreat."

This fellowship in synagogue service or religious meeting-houses, is the good old way from which we have gone astray. Read Luke 4:16-30; Acts 13:14-16; 1 Cor. 12, 13, 14; Psalm 22:22-26.

I did not tarry long in Hereford at this time. In business

matters, things looked gloomy, and so I resolved while I had the means, to leave. At this time I received word from my good friend, the doctor, enquiring if I would, to come to him to Kingston, Ireland. But I thought it not well to go at that time, and I have never heard from him since.

Before going further I will relate one little incident. I was requested to take the services at North Malvern, a distance of more than twenty miles. I left at 5 o'clock, Saturday afternoon, riding about seven miles with a Christian acquaintance, whether by stage or market waggon I cannot remember. At about 10 o'clock at night I came to the half-way houses between Hereford and Worcester. It was hot summer weather and I needed some refreshment. I had to go to the tavern. I prayed the Lord to direct me. I entered a large room well filled with men conversing in a neighborly way, having their mugs of ale and long clay pipes; so I thought I might get in a word to profit. C. H. Spurgeon had preached a sermon some time before, concerning the Saturday night of life; some of it was fresh in my mind. So I soon put on a little air of importance and said, "Gentlemen, I have a matter of great importance to communicate to you, if you will give me your attention for a minute or two." They could not tell what was coming—matters of state politics, business, or what. Pots and pipes were laid down and an amusing stare of curiosity came from the most of them. So I said that doubtless this hot weather and a week of hard work had made rest enjoyable, and some had the fruits of the toil in cash in their pockets; some were anticipating the rest of the morrow, and a blessing it is that we have a seventh day's rest, and are able to make good use of it. But the matter I wished to tell them of was concerning the Saturday night of life, and the wages paid for the toils of life, good or bad, and the eternal Sabbath that lay beyond, and as we cleaned up and got ready for the temporal so must we for the eternal, and it is by Jesus Christ we must enter the rest, and that this must have their serious attention.

As I rose to go, one said, We thank you very much. Another, We never heard anything better in our lives, will you drink with us? Another said, Pardon us intruding upon you, but you are late on the road. Are you going far? I answered, I am going to North Malvern and I have promised to be there by 12 o'clock. You will never get there, said they, and we all have comfortable homes and you are welcome to stay with any of us and go on in the morning. But I said, I have promised and I must try to keep my word, and I bade them farewell. As they said, I had a perplexing road to go; there were three roads running to a point and I knew not which was right or wrong, but the Lord brought me to the brother's door about the time I had stated.

I took dinner at the tavern on Monday. They told me the men were pleased with what I had said. Some may think it a very wicked thing to drink ale at 10 o'clock at night and especially on a Saturday; and also to eat bread and cheese at that hour is reckoned by some to be out of place. Our fathers drank ale for generations, many of them lived and died good, old men. The Mohammedans drink no wine but they allow no one to live but themselves, if they can help it.

If we would take our Christianity into the ale house rather than banter about prohibition it would be wiser, and if we had more Christian hospitality there would be less need of houses of entertainment. The gluttonous, drunken and idle son is sentenced by the law to be stoned. Parents, do your duty, and children, obey your parents in the Lord, for this is right.

Children cannot honor their parents by being idle, drunken, and profane. The Chinese law in making parents responsible for their children, might in some measure be well applied in this land. The scripture says, Wine is a mocker, and strong drink raging. He that is overcome thereby is not wise. It becomes the mocker and raging when men are overcome by it, and they that are overcome are unwise to say the least. Covetousness, oppression and pride are as hideous monsters as drunkenness. Yea, the family of these degenerates may be properly termed legion. They are of the brood of the prince of darkness. There are many who pride themself in having their pedigree on this line. I think I have understood that my parents once kept an ale house. They never were total abstainers but were of upright principles.

When I was about six or seven years of age I saw a large procession of total abstainers. My mother kept a small store, and among other things sold ginger beer at two cents per bottle. It was a hot day and I remember well many of the men turning in for ginger ale. But there were some who asked her for the brewers' ale. She said, You can't get that here, for what is got over the devil's back would surely go down his belly. This is true all round, but I have said more than I intended in starting, though I trust by God's blessing it may be profitable to some.

I left Hereford, stopping over to greet a Christian brother at Abergavenny. I was delighted with making his acquaintance at Hereford on my former visit. I had a great reverence for all who by word and deed declared themselves the Lord's; but many profess His name who lack the godly character. I was pleased to meet him once more, though busy in his market garden.

I was at this time deeply impressed with the consciousness of conflict in the Christian life, and the security of the believer in Christ, and as I neared the Bristol Channel, faith in God appeared to me the life-boat which though engulfed between the waves of trouble would in turn surely rise above them. The Lord knows and will provide, "He wings the arrow and guides the sparrow," as the following will show:

When I got to Newport the boat to Bristol was gone and I had to stay till next day, which took all my money but one copper beyond my fare. My trunk was at the station, and I could not tell how to get it to the boat. I was too weak to carry it, and I could find no other way; so I said, There is nothing else to do but to try, so I got it on my shoulder, and staggered along a little way, and dropped it on a hogshead, and as I dropped it a man said, Shall I carry your box? I said, I would be glad to get you to do so, but I cannot pay you. So he shouldered the trunk, saying, You have the price of a screw of tobacco, which meant a cent. He carried it to the boat, and I gave him the copper, saying, I am ashamed to offer it to you, but it is all that I have. He said, It will do for me, if it will do for you. I have nothing to do and I want a bit of tobacco to put in my pipe. So I thought, how wonderful is God's care.

A man in my trade carried on a Calvinist Close Baptist meeting in Bristol. I had made his acquaintance about a year before. He was a godly, wise, kindly, hospitable and well-instructed man, long since gathered to His people gone home, to be with Christ. The meeting-house bore the unostentatious name of Providence Chapel realizing that God had provided. Some of his sayings I remember well. One was that he could not understand what some persons were in the church for, unless it was to exercise the patience of others. Another was that he did not understand how godliness and covetousness go together. "We trust the Lord for the expenses of our meetings and have no collections. We ave a box at the door, they can put in or not as they please." · calling on him one day one of the members was telling him of a man preaching in the horse fair, concerning loving the Lord, so, said he, I asked him how it was we loved Him. He said, We love Him because He first loved us. I asked him if he would know him again. He said that he did not know; so I told him I was the person. I attended the Sunday evening service with this brother in Providence Chapel.

On my return I had a walk of about two miles to my parents' house. When I got there I was so exhausted, I said to my mother, My end is very near; I cannot live much longer. She wished me to see a medical man, but I reckoned from the past that the future would be no better. So I said, There is one sure remedy that I do know of, and that is to call for the elders of the church and have prayer and be anointed with oil in the name of the Lord, but I do not know where to find them. I would go for them if I knew where to find them, but I do not, but the Lord is true and can do His work without them, so let us have prayer and the oil, and I will anoint myself in His name. And we did so, for she did not want me to die, she was a woman of unfeigned faith as well as good judgment There was one trouble about it; she had on a silk dress, and the oil left some big patches on it. How they were taken out I never heard. I must say that to this day I have never experienced infirmity in the same way, nor of the same duration, and I must also say that in my case the promise by James is true. Blessed be God!

In the morning my mother wished me to go to her native village to see my brother and uncles. I stopped at Highbridge first, where I had spent many happy days among the Baptist brethren, during the second year of my conversion. I had been there at intervals for ten years before, having a cousin on my father's side residing there. I went to Cannington, my mother's native village, and held preaching in the street, and also in the town of Bridgewater, on the market, on the Cornhill. My uncle invited to tea a friend who was much interested in Christian work, and who directed me to go to Bath and make the acquaintance of a certain Christian brother there. He expressed a desire that some one would come to Bath to work in God's cause.

On Sunday I went over and expressed my willingness to work among them for a season, if agreeable to them. Before doing so I was very deeply impressed that I should do so. I held open-air services near the Abbey. At the first service I was invited to visit a sick woman, by her daughter. I did so.

Leaving them I spoke to two men who were grinding their tools. They made light of what I said. Turning from them to an old man who stood at a door listening to what had been said, in rural Somersetshire expression he said, "I be just seventy years auld, and I just bin a' thinking that I never bin to the communion in my life, and I bin a' thinking it was most time I did." So I inquired of his faith in Jesus Christ as his only and all-sufficient Saviour, and I found him well grounded in repentance towards God and faith in our Lord Jesus Christ. So I told him that Christ's Word taught first of all that they who believed in Him should be baptized like the eunuch who went down into the water, both Philip and the eunuch, or like our Saviour at thirty years of age who went down into the water and came straightway up out of the water, and that he was our example. He said, "I know that is right for I have read it in the Bible." "And I'll go too," said the old man. I found him so eager to do as the Lord's Word commanded, that I began to mistrust his sincerity, thinking that perhaps he did not rightly apprehend what I had said to him, although for myself I had been thoroughly convinced from the Scriptures of the straightway or forthwith baptism taught in it, as seen in connection with the Eunuch, the Apostle Paul, and the Philippian jailor and household, mentioned in the Acts of the Apostles.

I put off our aged friend, saying to him, I will call on you to-morrow, and if you are of the same mind as now I will go with you and baptize you as the Scripture commands. So the following day, Saturday, I visited him and found him as before. So I arranged to baptize him in the river which ran through the baths.

At the hour appointed I was there, but to my disappointment the candidate I could not find, so I concluded that my former thought was right—that he had more talk than character. After waiting nearly an hour I started to leave, when I met the brother, who hailed me with, "Where have he bin; I thought you was never a'coming." I accordingly baptized him. But, strange to say, though I had baptized about fifty persons before, in the immersion, I omitted to pronounce the Lord's name in connection with the act of immersion. Although the whole work had been done in the Lord's name, in prayer, supplication and thanksgiving which had preceded it, I had to acknowledge to our friend that I had not pronounced the Lord's name in connection with the baptism, so he said, Let us do it right, and I immersed him a second time. Coming out of the water he entered the bath and thanked the Lord for His mercy to him in leading him in His own right way, for Jesus' sake. I parted his company and did not meet him again for twelve months, it being Saturday and the next day being an exceedingly wet one.

I left the city on Monday and went to Bristol, then to Cheltenham, Worcester, and Malvern, to fill promises previously made to friends.

A little incident marked the goodness and care of the Lord. As I was about to enter Cheltenham, I was met by a young man of respectable appearance and manner, who asked me to help him to obtain a lodging, as he was going to Gloucester, but was without money. I had but fourpence half penny. I thought I am going to Cheltenham to those I know, and he is going to Gloucester where he knows no one, and I can better do without money than he can. So I emptied my pocket, giving him the little I had.

Calling on a Christian sister, I was asked to tea and to stay for the night. After tea she said, I have been thinking of you for some time, and am sure you must be needing money, and gave me $10.00, more than twenty times what I had given. I said to myself, The Lord soon returned me my four and a half pence.

I tarried in Cheltenham for a few days, visiting a few Christian persons, went on to Worcester and then to Malvern, visiting some of my acquaintances, one being an infirm Christian woman with whom I had previously spoken concerning her being baptized in the Lord's name. Hitherto she had raised strong objections to it, but during the four months or more of my absence, she must have reflected on what I had said to her, or upon the subject, for when I now spoke to her she surprised me by saying that she was ready to be baptized. It was up in the hills where water was difficult to be obtained, and the bath for baptizing must have the water carried by hand, from a distant spring. She expressed herself ready to be baptized the following week, but upon reflecting, I had to acknowledge to her that my conscience was not at ease, for the Scripture said, "They were baptized the same day and the same hour." So I told her that it was not right to propose next week when the Scripture said, "The same day and the same hour," for I knew not what a day or hour might bring forth. I asked if she would be ready to-day if I could arrange, and she said she was.

I attempted to do so, but could not get the bath filled at the appointed time. Several of the brethren and sisters came from Worcester, and at the little meeting-house in the orchard, she was baptized, after which we joined together in remembering the Lord in the breaking of bread—the only time I remember doing so except on the first day of the week.

Some persons think and say that to do as I have now related, is an innovation of good order, but this is the order of human invention. "The commandments of the Lord stand fast forever, and the thoughts of His heart to all generations," and the Apostle Paul has written, "Whatsoever ye have seen, or heard, or received of me, do, and the God of peace shall be with you." Obedience is better than sacrifice.

After this I returned to Cheltenham and carried on services in the town and out of it, a number expressed a desire to be baptized in the Lord's name, some desired to make a parade of it, from which some wrangling followed. I ceased to receive their support and hospitality, preferring to work with my hands and be free from the disagreeable bondage of dogmatism, petty condescension and paltry liberality. But in this I doubtless made a mistake, for I had received word that if I went to Birmingham I should have opportunity to go in and out among Christian brethren, while working for the Master. Also it was in my heart and mind to return to Liverpool, but I continued for a while in Cheltenham preaching in the open air two or three times a week, as well as in cottage prayer services. I sought the use of the baptisteries of two Baptist churches, but in vain. But I obtained the use of a very large and handsome bath, belonging to a hydropathic physician. Among those baptized while there was one who was to be my future wife. Others went to Worcester to be baptized.

I arrived at Birmingham the day that the Prince Consort died, Dec. 14th, 1861, and strange to say, on my previous visit to Birmingham, 1852, the Duke of Wellington died.

I found the brethren with whom I thought to stay in Birmingham at variance, and not being able to judge between right and wrong, the two champion preachers saying hard things of each other, I again worked at my trade, and in the London & Northwestern railway shops, had the following experience:

Some forty or fifty of us took our breakfasts in a messroom provided by the Company. As my Bible was my constant companion my spare minutes were filled with reading it. While others read the daily newspapers, and that aloud, I also was asked to read the Scriptures. Finding a number agreeable, I did so, and some endured it for a while, but after several mornings one man in a pet got on his feet, saying, "This is no place for Bible reading; if you want to read the Bible, do so at home." Then came a hot debate, another saying, "We have to listen to men fights, cock fights, dog fights and a lot more disgraceful things from the daily papers," and his sentence was, that if the Bible could not be read the newspaper could not be read; so there was a strong division in the camp, and they made things hotter for me than I could stand, so I packed up my tools and took myself away. Some literary, Biblical dignities of oratorical renown, told me it was pushing religion down men's throats, and thought themselves wise in reproving such liberty. But I had to find afterwards that the same could lie and stand to it, so I had to let them go with the reproof they merited, and I have not as yet heard of any change.

1862. In the month of January, 1862, I was married, in Birmingham.

I did a little open-air preaching in Birmingham amid some strife, and then went in the providence of God to Wolverhampton, some twelve or more miles distant. Reflecting upon my stay in Birmingham, I concluded that in the Lord's work I had been very negligent while there, and determined for the future to be more diligent. So on the first night in Wolverhampton, I saw a large crowd of men in the centre of the town, which was a large opening, I thought, here is work that can be done, and I commenced single-handed to proclaim as best I could the everlasting Gospel. But I very soon found myself in the hands of the police and taken to the station. He appeared to me to be a reprobate. I said to him, My friend, it appears to me that if you had your Saviour here you would deal with him as you are dealing with me, and in his ignorance and madness he said he would do so to Him or anyone else. At the station I stayed while the profane and drunken were being tumbled in, and I felt sick at thinking to have to house with such company. At last my landlord came and became security for my appearing in court next day, when I was sentenced to a fine of ten shillings and costs which would be together about four dollars, or half a fortnight in jail, or to promise not to offend again. I had written on the past night to Birmingham to the zealous advocates of Primitive Christianity, and they, like the goody people of the town, left me to myself to pay the fine, or go to jail as I thought best. Not even a post card or a telegram or anything of the kind came for my encouragement. As I had gone to the fight prompted by good will and obedience to God's commands to preach the Gospel to every creature, the duly appointed representatives of organized religion had no interest in an itinerant Christian street preacher going to jail as a recompense for his labors. But while I hesitated to take jail— the condition of my parentless wife occasioned it—the news reporters in court tried to act in their measure, the good Samaritan, and they whispered to me, "Promise him, promise him." So they awakened a bit of amusement in me, and jesuit-like I said to myself, I'll not go there, but I'll go somewhere else. So I was let off, though I had resolved to take some other stand— one of the statements against me being that the crowd was large, and a runaway horse might have caused serious trouble. Personally I would rather have gone to jail than have had the gloom I experienced outside the court, because I did not stand firm and go to jail—God knows how far I was right or wrong.

However, before dinner there came to me at the shop a good man who expressed his regret at what I had experienced, and told me that the enmity I had experienced in my good endeavor was only a repetition of experiences others had gone through before me, and said he would find me a spot where I should not be meddled with. So he got me a stand upon the troughs of the canal, and there I spoke without hinderance. I was reminded of the circumstance four years later and about two hundred miles from the place, by a man who had seen what had taken place on the occasion, so I suppose these little testimonies have had some influence for good, though they may have been much despised by many at the time. It is written, Where the word of a king is there is power. So the words of the King Eternal, Immortal and Invisible, the Only Wise God cannot fail, however feeble the instrument that sounds it forth, God's choice being the weak things of this world and things despised, yea and things that are not, to bring to naught things that are, that no flesh should glory in His presence. 1 Cor. 1:27-29.

I made an effort to return to Liverpool from here; but the American war had so stopped trade that the employer I had worked for in Liverpool advised me not to come as I probably would not find employment. I went to Manchester in the hope of making a stand there, but could not obtain the work or wages I was looking for. I felt free from any obligation to return to Liverpool as desired when I left, as I could not find a way open, and after my past experience I determined I would not commit myself to any, lest they should say to me as Nabal did to David when he wanted bread, There are many servants now-a-days that break away every one from his master; and he gave him not. 1 Sam. 25:10.

In the midst of my desire to reach the people I longed for a rural life, and the city of Hereford, with the rich pasture, magnificent timber and its beautiful river had so entwined itself in my imagination that I felt I could live and labor there in contentment if the way should be open, and so in the providence of God for a few months it was. I preached regularly in the open air, and here the police preserved order for me. I labored in and round the city and country for a few months, but found it was not to be my resting place.

I returned to my native town, and my good Bro. Hicks, a Gadsby Baptist preacher, who himself labored at his trade, or rather was foreman in the factory in which I worked, related his experience in former years, in the same neighborhood. He had been dissatisfied in the place in which he labored, which was somewhere near Gloucester, and thinking that the neighborhood of Shrewsbury some sixty or more miles distant, would be more suitable for him, he started for it. Sixty or more years ago communication from town to town was not as easily made as now. When he got into the town the words continually rang in his ears, Elijah, what doest thou here, and not being able to return a suitable answer to the voice calling from within his heart, without stopping to see about business he immediately returned to the place he had left.

This good brother had, in his early days, seen many changes and gone through many difficulties, and by these trials as well as by grace, was ready to console and encourage others in affliction. For many years he had been preacher at a little meeting-house called Providence Chapel, and his abode was called Zoar Cottage, adjoining it, which was characteristically named (near to flee unto), a little of the declining shadow of Puritan times; would there were more of it! He labored with his hands and preached the Word, and there were no collections at his meetings. It was a work of faith and a labor of love. He said on one occasion, We have a box at the door for contributions, I do not judge any, whether they give or not, but I do not know, he said, how covetousness and the grace of God can go together.

He was liberal-souled, for when I got to town he brought me half a sovereign ($2.50) unsought for, and later when two men in the trade from London came to me on tramp, looking for work, whom I housed for the time, he brought them five shillings to start them again on the road. This good brother has passed into rest and his works do follow him, and the same will be to us if we follow in the same path.

In November of the year 1862, I purposed to go again to London. I had lived with a godly and somewhat remarkable woman, my parents' home being at the other end of the town. She had belonged to the English Church at Plymouth under the pastorate of a Mr. Hawker. In this church first began the association of Brethren, known as Plymouth Brethren. They were called a church within the church, and finally they left the English Church and became a separate company. She was among the early members and was baptized in the sea at the age of 12 years before Muller and Craig had joined the company. This good woman was desirous that I should remain in Bristol, and as I was about to leave she said, You must be mad, to think of leaving for London at this time of the year. But I had no thought about times, good or bad. I concluded that the Lord's goodness reached all the year round, so that I was not much frightened or hurt however things went; but I did not like her saying I was mad, neither did I want to get into more trouble than I could get easily through, so I went to my bedroom, and taking my Bible from my pocket, I prayed the Lord to direct me by His Word. I read down the 71st Psalm and halted at the 16th verse, "I will go in the strength of the Lord God, I will make mention of thy righteousness, even of thine only." That word never came to me with such force before. Then I said, Perhaps it means someone else and it does not apply to me.

Here I would say that all the Scriptures apply first to Christ, and then to His people, they being members of His body, but Christ the Head, as well as the Alpha and Omega which takes in the whole body. At that time I could not take out of this passage the assurance which I needed, but that was my shortsightedness and want of faith, for it more than covered the ground. So I read on to Psalm 72:12. "For He shall deliver the needy when he crieth; the poor also, and him that hath no helper." That fitted exactly my circumstances and conditions, and I could triumphantly say, Enough, my gracious Lord; my faith can on this promise live, can on this promise die; and with a school-boy's jump I went down the stairs and said, Farewell, it is all right, I am off, and away went my wife and I.

I paid the friends a visit in Bath, and saw the good old man I had baptized fourteen months before. They said he was soul-prospering, so I hailed him cheerily in the Master's name, and he responded by getting down his Bible and telling me how much comfort he had gotten out of this and the other. I suppose I had prayer with him, and left, not letting him know who I was. I suppose it was with him then as it is with me now, I do not remember faces and forms as· readily as I used to. I was well pleased with the unfeigned faith the good old man displayed.

I had not been back with my good friends long when tugging up the hill came the old gentleman, and taking hold of my hand he said, "I thought I'd die and never see ye. I come to thank ye for the help you have been to me," and he left a shilling in my hand. This meant much from a poor, aged man. He has long since died, but I heard of his continuing a good life and making a joyful end.

From Bath I received a commendation to brethren in London, thinking I might do good service for the Master there. My wife remaining for a while in Bath. I did not find the reception in London over genial; in fact, I preferred to work at the trade rather than have their professed support and liberality. and at my earliest withdrew to another part of London. They afterwards came with legal constraint for me to return, and I simply said I could do with them, or without them, but as I discerned little grace and big show, that would not do for me, and I immediately rented a place and fixed it up for service, with but little success, but I made a few acquaintances and for a time we worked harmoniously. A few professed conversion, but, like the Samaritans of old, and many of to-day, they feared the Lord and served idols.

I baptized a few persons in the canal, baths, and in Shouldheim St. Baptist Church. Mr. Dike, I think, was the name of the pastor who gave me a welcome to use it at any time, but I concluded it was not to much profit to baptize persons who largely acted as if that ordinance ended their obligations to God and His Word. "If any man draw back," said Paul, "my soul hath no pleasure in him." However, to his own Master every man standeth or falleth.

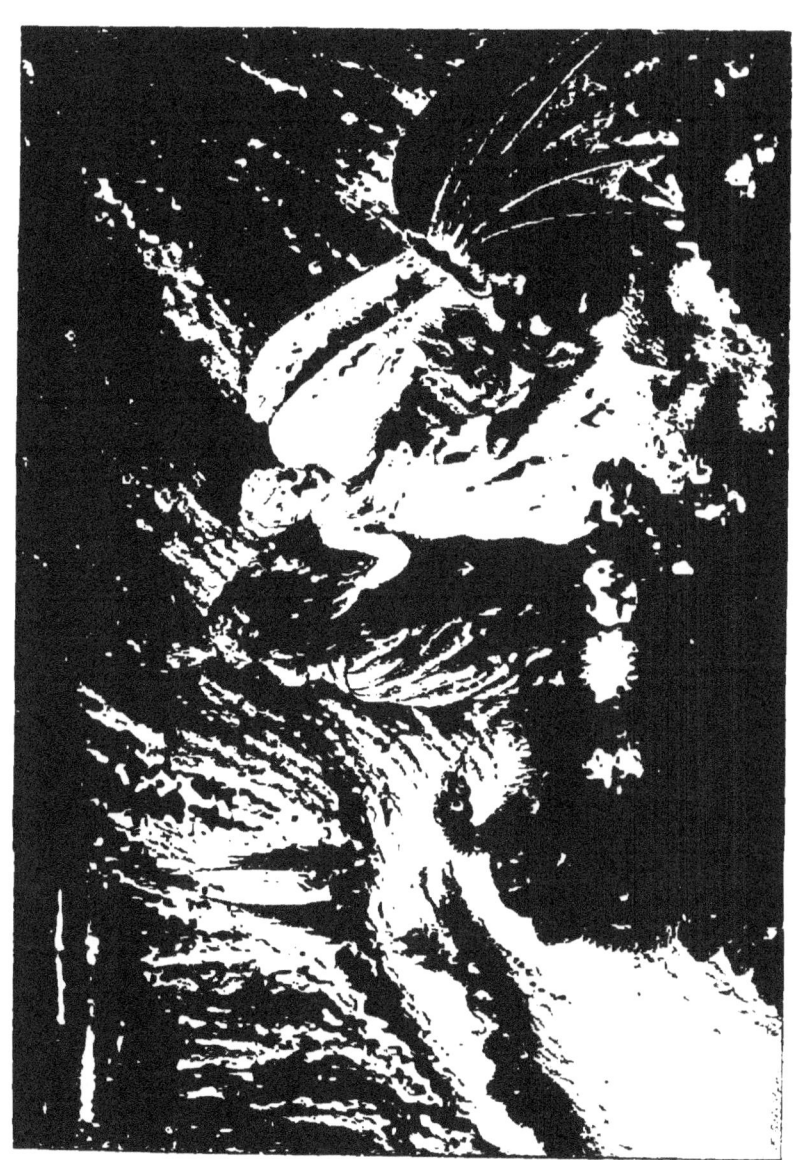

"They tried hard to get hold of her." (See page 34.)

I was early impressed with the word: "Whereunto ye have attained, walk by the same rule, minding the same things." So I have endeavored to keep my face Godward and the rest could go as it would. I did much preaching on the renowned Paddington green until the Jesuital workers had it fenced in with iron rails, and prohibited persons from standing and talking together. They made it look very artistic with flowers, but killed out the Christian life and godly activity of the scene.

I will here relate an incident that should never be forgotten, religiously, socially, or politically. There had been, a few years previous to this, disturbances at open air meetings in Hyde Park, on account of some sympathy being expressed for Garabaldi in his struggle for Italian liberty which occasioned dissatisfaction on the part of the Pope's supporters. Hitherto the Park had been common ground for all comers. (I also having in years past planned in my mind to preach the Gospel there, with a band, but feebleness of health hindered me.) The Romanist rowdies occasioned Hyde Park to be closed against all preaching and lecturing and meetings of all kinds until 1866 and 1867. Paddington Green was the second edition of their manoeuvering to shut men's mouths, but how true the old saying is, "God is above the devil."

In Sept., 1886, some political agitation determined to try the strength of the authorites to hinder them holding their meetings in the open air in Hyde Park; the police force was called out to hold the fort for the Romanist schemers, which ended in a big fight and many going to the lockup. They began to talk about hanging the rioters. What geese and gobblers these sanctimonious characters are. In the following March, the little band of 500 political agitators gathered to possess themselves of the right of occupation of the Park for free speech. The government maintained the blockade by placing in the Park two companies or regiments of the line, and one company of artillery. This made things look serious, and the whole country was agitated. But one of the agitators was a lawyer who understood his business, and would stand to his guns. The little company gathered at Trafalgar Square, marched to and entered the Park and held their meeting, though the bayonets and guns were there, and the way remains open to the public for freedom of speech to the present time. The secret came out afterwards that at midnight the government had called the best legal advisors to enquire what could be done according to law, and found that they could not prevent them from entering the park, except for misdemeanor, and that without violence, upon pain of being tried for manslaughter, and if they would bring any to justice they must serve each one with a summons at his own house. So the Home Secretary to be quit of his folly, next day retired from office. Christ, not England alone, expects every man to do his duty.

1864. After closing my first meeting room I obtained the loan of the Cabman's Hall on Bell St., Paddington, and held there some encouraging services. I had a large half sheet bill printed, announcing the services. This was in 1864. One of the bills I put over my bench at which I worked. My employer, while on his rounds through the shop, read the bill. Days and weeks would go by sometimes without his coming close to me. On this occasion he said, Buskin, you are a foolish man. You cannot do this preaching and mind your business, too. Why, if I should do as you do, my business would go to the dogs. I said, There is a difference, sir, between you and me. I believe God, and you do not. So he said, That won't do, I am not an infidel, I go to church and we have a very good minister, and if I do as he says I shall not be far wrong. But you can never do this preaching and your business, too. Now, said he, I will give you a bit of good advice. You let this preaching go till you can find a man with money, then let him find the money and you do the preaching; then you will be all right. But if I had taken his advice I should have waited a long time and done nothing.

I have been looking out from that day to this, now nearly thirty-four years, and the man, his shadow or ghost, has not as yet overtaken me, though I have hunted for him more than for most men, from Her Majesty's Privy Counsellors downward, and have not found him or her, but this I have learned, that I cannot go from the presence of the Lord or flee from His Spirit; therefore I have present with me Him who has all power in heaven and in earth, and He is better to me than a host with all their treasures and all their force and He has promised that He will supply all our needs. It is for every one to undertake the duties that are before him, or in other words, "Whatsoever thy hand findeth to do, do it with thy might," and do all in the name of Jesus, to the glory of God.

This employer felt kindly toward me, and when I thought of leaving London to go to the eastern counties, thinking that he would buy out a business, he offered me, in the event of his doing so, that I should take charge of it for him. But I had no desire for such bondage, and prayed that I might be freed from it, and it was so.

While in his employ one of the men became sick with smallpox. His case was very dangerous. Many suffered and died at that time in London. He lay for three weeks before the disease turned, and I was constrained by the circumstances of his wife and small children to do what I could to help them, as one of the children also was suffering from the disease. I sat up with him five nights out of eight, doing also my daily work and open-air preaching twice on Sundays and once in the week. I think my watching him was the means of preserving his life, for sometimes I had to keep him in bed by physical force. One man near by in the height of the disease, got out of bed and pumped water on himself and died.

The effects of this exercise reduced me to a condition of weakness that I never before nor since experienced. One day at the shop, I could not work. I sat on my tool chest and was overtaken with fainting, but I could hear the men saying, He has got the disease all right. How I got home I do not now remember, but I was so weak that it was a continual pain to sit, stand or lie, and every passing thought within me would act with a shock of pain from the crown of my head to the sole of my feet. But after three days I was able to go again to the shop, and not the least sign of smallpox. The poor man recovered, but much disfigured, and after a visit to the convalescent home by the sea side, returned ruddy and strong. The Lord preserved me from being at all affected by the disease. There is a difference between no fear in duty and reckless defiance when in danger. The Lord has promised to keep us in our going out and coming in, and personally I have proved it, but I have suffered much from weakness.

About this time I had to hold service in the Cabman's Hall, Victoria Station, near Buckingham Palace, another person taking my place at the Bell St. Cabman's Hall, Paddington. It was about two miles distant, but before service was ended I fell from the desk to the floor in a faint. I had experienced many such turns in former years, and that was the last I think till I came to this country, and only once here. I did not continue the meeting long at Bell St. Some made objections against my Sunday morning services which were for Christian fellowship and worship, and as the hall was loaned and not hired I had to leave. I was afterwards offered the possession of a hall near the Marylebone theatre which was not far away, but I was afraid of a second edition of Bell mission, and did not accept it.

About this time the adversaries of Christian liberty, closed up Paddington Green, that no religious services should be held there, as they had previously done at Hyde Park. In both places persons gathered by hundreds and thousands, on Sundays, and sometimes week days, to preach and hear the Gospel, and some to oppose. The most lawless opposers were the Romanists, and some amusing experiences took place by the opposition of professed infidels as well as many a logical debate. A doctor sometimes would come from near Reading, a distance of forty miles, to attend these services, and sometimes to teach; he was a benevolent man with some peculiar doctrines. I know he was strongly opposed to eating pork and rabbits. When first he was brought to me he declared himself to be a preacher of the Gospel, an evangelist. He took tea with me. But for his appearance, I thought he did not fare amiss, compared with the Master who had not where to lay his head. He was gentlemanly, but homely. His garments were not gay but very good, and I thought him somewhat a novel representative of the Master. Not wishing to misjudge his words or his appearance, I presented a half crown for his acceptance for the Master's sake. He laughed, and said, My brother, I can buy you and all your houses. But I think he made a mistake, for figures are high in that line with me. However he pressed me to accept a half sovereign for the poor who were with me, which I did not refuse, for I had a few pets of that kind. Bro. Joseph Bell was one, a strong Calvinist Baptist, whom I can never forget, and about whom I will have a few things to say to profit. Some time later the doctor brought from the Midland Counties to Paddington Green, a converted pugilist, to preach the Gospel, and as he talked about the Bible, one of the champion professors of infidelity, defiantly said he did not believe the Bible. The pugilist said to him, I'll prove you a liar in quick time. Will you answer a few questions? Tell me, do you think you will ever die? "I should be a fool to think that I would not die," said the man. "And does not the Bible tell you so?" said the pugilist. So the infidel was knocked out at the first blow and retired, and the people laughed at the simple manner in which he was beaten. Poor brother Bell. He was despised and afflicted, but he was a happy soul and always ready to speak the praises of the Lord; a shoemaker by trade, but his infirmity did not allow him to earn his bread by it. The Scripture says, "The poor is hated even of his own neighbor." So was Joseph. One man with whom I dealt, a baptized believer, said to me, If you knew the character of that Joseph Bell you would not have so much to do with him. What is the trouble, I said. Do you know, said he, he has carried the sign boards round town for the infidels? I said, That is a serious matter. Yes, said he, I don't want you to take my word without evidence, I'll send you to one of the infidels who will tell you the same. So the next day, I suppose, I went to see the infidel. When I got there we knew each other, having had some debating on Paddington Green. He welcomed me in, and inside the front door hung a Scripture roll of daily texts. I said the first thing, I see you are not as much of an unbeliever as you profess. He said, That's the wife's, and I don't interfere with her. So the Lord had doubtlessly given him a good wife and she was trying quietly to lead him to God. I said to him, Is it true that Joseph Bell carried the board for meetings of your society? Oh, yes, he did, but give the old man his due; he afterwards came to the meeting and said all he could against us. Good for Bro. Bell, I thought. I thanked my infidel neighbor and started to discipline Bro. Joseph. I suppose he was with my wife waiting to have tea with us. I said to him very seriously, Bro. Bell, a very grave charge has been made concerning you. Yes, yes, said he, what is it? I heard that you have been employed by the infidels to carry the advertising boards of their meetings round town; is it true? He said, Yes I did, and who told you? I said, Bryant. Miserable fellow, he said, he stopped to lecture to me about it and I told him I was getting a half crown or 60c for doing it and I needed it, and if he liked to give me the money I did not want to carry the board. And did he tell you what was on it? No, said I, what was it? "The Bible, was it true or false; an open question." Why, you could have carried such a board as that, couldn't you? So I had to laugh, telling him what the infidel had already said to me. This shows how some persons who are not actuated by love, if they can find a little hole to get their mischievous fingers into, will do their best to make a big rent, then think they are very wise.

After this poor Bro. Bell sent for me one Sunday to see him; he had fallen on the street in a faint, and his doctor passing, ordered him to be taken to Marylebone workhouse hospital. I immediately went, and seeing him I said, Bro. Bell, how are you? Calvinist-like in a whisper, he said, The Lord found me in the wilderness yesterday, but bless the Lord I am on the rock now. I am very weak and my throat is dry; bring me a little wine. I sent it the next day by my wife, but he had passed over the river of death. His sorrows and sufferings were ended. I went with his wife and son to the grave. A sad and humiliating sight is the deadhouse of Marylebone hospital. A dozen or more corpses lay waiting for burial. In a deep down grave of 15 feet or more, Bro. Bell and others were laid, and somewhere near the same grave lies a dear little son of mine, Samson by name, buried when I was away from home, and my hope and comfort is, "We shall meet again on the resurrection morning when the shadows shall have passed away and life's eternal day shall bring no more sorrow or decay."

Time went on and I wanted more effectually to carry on work for the Master, but found it difficult to do so. There was little fellowship of the heart and spirit. Fellowship of words and forms and display, rigid sanctimoniousness and preciseness of religious pronunciation and accent, but little brotherly love. I held open-air meetings in the outskirts of London, Harrow, and Kilburn, where I also had a meeting room, but little was accomplished. I occasionally attended the operative Christian Association on Church St., Paddington. This was sustained by the rich in the interest of the working classes, and here I found more simplicity of heart and character than elsewhere. One of the members became sick and finally lost his reason and tried to destroy himself in various ways, the last being by starving himself. I occasionally visited him at Hanwell asylum, taking a journey of six or eight miles to get there, and it was a pitiable sight to see the hundreds of lunatics of various characters, some fierce, some feeble, simple, cunning, and some sane. To a young woman I remarked concerning her father, that there did not appear to be anything the matter with him. She said he was all right while there, but as soon as he had his liberty he was uncontrollable. One man made many statements to me to convince me that he was allied to the Royal Family of England, and just to get rid of him he was placed there and there was no insanity about him. On one occasion the wife of the man I used to go to see, gave me a cake and pudding to take to him to induce him to eat, but while he appeared perfectly reasonable on all matters, it was in vain that I tried to get him to eat. Concerning the cake he could not touch it for it was not paid for, and the Scripture said, "Owe no man anything," and he would make no move from that, and concerning the pudding, if he ate that unworthily he would be condemned; so I had to leave him as I found him.

On my former visit he wished to have my Bible in which I had written the hymn which I suppose was then new: "My Jesus, I love Thee, I know Thou art mine." So I asked him concerning the Bible, but he said the men liked the hymn so well that they stole the Bible from him to have the hymn. On my return I told the association that the only hope for his deliverance was by prayer to God, in which they earnestly united, and his abstinence was overcome and the next visit I paid, he was so far recovered as to be able to work in the garden, and finally he was restored to his home.

1866. In the year 1866 my strength gave out, and though I had labored in London from Nov. '62, to June '66, I had little satisfaction from my hard labors. Christian fellowship was largely only a name, and I wished to be away. In May or June the large money panic took place in London. T. e banks and houses failed for £100,000,000, but the Providence of God had provided for me Scarboro, the renowned seaside summer resort, and there I was from June to November. My health was restored and my employment was comparatively profitable. I held open-air services on the sea beach and in the open places of the town.

I sailed from London with my wife and family on the steamship Bruser. A month later she sank at midnight and fourteen persons were drowned, she being cut nearly in two by a Sunderland coaler. In a lumber camp twenty-five years later, while distributing tracts I had one entitled the Steamship Bruser. So I read it myself. The writer stated that in it he related his experience on board the ship at the time, to be an encouragement to any Christian who may be in dread of the hour of death. He said the Captain woke him out of his sleep, telling him to save himself for the ship was going down. He rushed to the deck in his shirt and drawers but could find no way of escape. He then followed another man up the rigging, the first man trying to reach from the one yard arm to the other, fell, whether drowned or not he could not say, he saw that for him there was no hope of escape. He then concluded that in a few minutes he should be under the water and life ended. When things had been well with him he had rejoiced in God, and he asked himself, could he now do the same and leave his wife and children to his heavenly Father's care? Immediately he began to sing, "Rock of Ages," or "Jesus, lover of my soul."

He had no further care but immediately there was a rush down the deck and he ran down the rigging and then found himself safe in a boat. God gives the grace in the needed hour. To me this tract had a double interest, the instruction it gave and the incident which had caused me especially to be thankful to God for His preserving care over me and mine. The weathee was remarkably fine but the trouble was caused by a mistake in the lights.

At Scarboro I made my first acquaintance with Christadelphians, but they largely reminded me of wax figures of Madame Tasand, of London, with beautiful figure, moving eyes, and measured motion, but lacking the fruits of the Spirit, love, joy peace, meekness, gentleness, etc. We get the heavy dong of Big Ben the Cathedral bell, of St. Paul's, London, sometimes heard a distance of 20 miles, and the harmonious, silvery sound of the clanging chimes, pealing sacred sounds, and including all that comes between the two, and so much of the profession is as mechanical and dead as all the belfry bells. To be understood aright it says that life is far from here, and like sea bells should be better understood to say, Beware of rocks and shoals, and loss and death. Nothing will suffice but the Spirit of life in Christ Jesus dwelling in us and our being led thereby and the Word of Christ dwelling in us in all wisdom.

I went again to Bristol, my native town, having a strong infatuation for rural life, although for town life to me there is none to compare with London, but the charm and din and the whirl carries you through the distance of its streets, and you have quickly to find the physical force exhausted by the labor and excitement of London life. Here again I conducted open-air Gospel preaching, and among other places took for my stand a position on the wharf near the drawbridge where many times before I had held such and saw others do the same. I had not long been there when I was ordered away by a policeman who said it was prohibited. I said that I had known services to have been held there for many years, and that it was in no way interfering with business or passengers, and for these reasons I refused to leave, also considering the authority of heaven to exceed the authority of earth. I was taken to the police station and debated the matter with the Inspector or Chief of Police. I told him it was a Christian duty to do so, that there was evident need of such work, and that I could remember that such work had been done there from my early childhood, twenty-five years before. He said it was now prohibited and that if I wanted to preach, Brandon Hill was the place. I said to him, Sir, it is poor evidence of wisdom on the part of the officer who has charge of this city to tell me to preach to the winds on Brandon Hill, where at night no people are passing. He said, You cannot preach at the drawbridge unless you have a special permit from the mayor; but as this counsel did not proceed from the doctrines of God's Word, I did not follow it, but went elsewhere and was not again interfered with.

I learned that the cause had been that Romanists had made a clamouring while men were preaching there, and that one man had been thrown into the water of the harbor. This was another evidence that instead of the authorities being a terror to evil-doers and for the praise of those who do well, they suppressed the right to accommodate the wrong. Strange that men should be sent from Christian lands to that of the heathen to do the very thing that they are prohibited from doing in the Christian lands from which they are sent.

1869. Failing to realize what I expected, in business matters, I returned to London early in 1869 to find things in confusion as a result of the money panic of '66. I had not felt much of it, but in London things were low, and I concluded I would(D. V.) try Canada, so I went to Liverpool and then to Ireland, intending to sail from Ireland. I did not find opportunity for out of door preaching during the six months I was there, but I did find much pleasure in the fellowship with a few godly souls.

I saw some rioting in Newry at the time of the Amnesty meeting; on Sunday the constabulary charged through the streets with fixed bayonets, (which were something new to me) while at the same time one well dressed and orderly young man was bleeding freely from a long gash down the side of his face, and all this was the outcome of rival religions—not Christianity.

In Dublin I was present at a Bible reading at the Y.M.C.A., one of the most enjoyable to me that I ever was at. Old and young alike took part, and I thoguht grace was very manifest among them. At Killashandra, near Cavan, I had an enjoyable intercourse with some Roman Catholic families, one having joined with me in prayer and Scripture reading, in Kilkenny. I also made the acquaintance of some godly persons whose delight was in the Lord and His Word.

At Waterford I was astonished to see a woman kneeling down in the open air and public highway to a black image. That may be called Christian, but rightly it may be said of it,

"The heathen in his blindness bows down to wood and stone." I saw also the round tower, built by Strongbow, Earl of Bristol, and his associates in the twelfth century, being then used as a police barracks. The river and surrounding scenery there is very beautiful.

1870. I sailed for Liverpool and there took boat for Bristol where I remained till June (1871) and then sailed for Canada, to seek there that which I failed to find satisfactory in England, Wales or Ireland—the opportunity and ability to effectually carry on the work of God's grace. The Monkish system of priestcraft so largely pervades all classes of constituted religiousness, that to be honest they might put up over their doors, "Outsiders need not apply, who will not subscribe to our Authorized Constitutional program." Thus you get it from Romanism down to Quakerism, Brethrenism, etc., in 500 different forms, and apart from these compacts, scarcely two can be found to walk together in the liberty and power of God's Holy Spirit; they must be tarred in some way or other that they maybe known as the sheep of the degeneracy. How long before the time will come that they shall call every man his neighbor under the vine and under the fig tree, apart from the Pope's potentates, petty presidents and officially bloated men in office, who, in order to maintain their official dignity would, like the Jews, prescribe to Jesus Christ himself. The times and circumstances may be different, but the fashion and spirit that actuates, is the same. The perverted spirit begins with infancy, and gets hardened, dried up, and destitute of feeling with old age, and the young, full blown with their officiousness and zeal, are often the embodiment of impertinence, instead of godly graciousness. How quickly young men get from industrious callings to strutting around as religious fops, with their religious garbs and canes, and their affected clerical sanctity of palaver and manner, instead of being stalwart and diligent men of righteousness, forgetful or wilfully negligent of, the biblical admonishings against such conduct.

It was in my mind to provide a home for my family in Canada, so that I could be the more free to pursue Christian work. I was grieved on account of the number of men in England who could not obtain employment, and the difficulty to obtain a proper remunerative price for labor and manufactured goods, so I concluded that by leaving I should make room for someone else. Being unwell at the time I concluded that a sailing ship would be better than a steamship.

1871. On the 25th of June, 1871, I left Liverpool for Quebec, with my wife and four children. I think the name of the ship was Minerva. After eight days a heavy storm arose. I held religious services both Sundays and week days, and also had prayer on the deck at Liverpool before leaving. The second Sunday was spent by many in playing cards, as many godless ones were on board, but on Monday, before breakfast, a heavy wave struck the ship, which caused the death of one man, and his wife returned from Quebec to England a widow. I went to the deck to see the cause of the crash. Things were terribly knocked about. The captain saved one man from being washed away; another told me he was carried away by a wave and did not know whether he was in the sea or on the vessel. The man who died had his legs and back broken.

The storm lasted several days and our hope of living through it was very small. I had prayer among the passengers. Some ungodly ones were led with tears to cry to God for sparing mercy. An Irish widow, with a little son, with joyful countenance, said to me, "If the ship goes down we shall be with the Lord. What a blessing." The storm subsided; the poor man was buried in the sea; I conducting the religious service. Two weeks later, on Saturday evening, in a fog, the ship ran upon the rocks, on St. Paul's Island, in the Gulf of St. Lawrence. Providentially we escaped with our lives, but lost much of our goods. For eight days we remained on the island. Our money and many valuables were lost. We landed in Quebec six days later, about the 3rd of August.

I had intended remaining in Quebec, but owing to the wreck I went to Toronto; but failing to find suitable employment I went to Hamilton where I worked for a short time at the western Car Works, but came near death from the tapeworm. However I was kindly and effectually treated at the hospital by Dr. O'Rilley.

1872. I remained in Hamilton until April, 1872, then went to London to work at the Car Works, but as I could not come to terms I went to St. Thomas and worked on the Canada Southern Railroad. During this time I ceased my public activities in Christian work by reason of the discouragements I had met and some of the difficulties I had to encounter.

1873. In July, 1873, I left St. Thomas for Toronto intending to go to Muskoka to take up land, so that I might be free to work in the Gospel as soon as I could fix up a home for my family. In the fall of this year, a sore grief to myself and wife was the death of our daughter about seven months old. I could not understand it,' I could not see a cause and was led to open my Bible to look for instruction and consolation. I opened at the Book of Job chapters 7 and 14 where I found comfort. She is almost as vividly before me now as she was when alive. I wrote the following for her grave:

Thou art resting, dearest infant, thy pain and struggles o'er;
Thou hast fulfilled thy work, the days of God's appointed score,
But thy young heart and death-closed eyes shall yet in light and life revive
On the blessed morn when the dead from earth shall rise,
For in the dark and silent grave the Shepherd's voice shall sound,
The lambs He'll gather with his arm and on His breast they shall rejoice,
Forever saved from sorrow, death and hell.

This was true consolation which but for God's Word I should not have known or had brought to mind. It also set me to thinking more seriously, and working more earnestly than I had. I opened my door for social prayer, though very few came, but that matters very little; they and only they who wait on the Lord renew their strength.

Some time after this I went one Sunday to Queen's Park, and spoke with some measure of acceptance concerning God's grace. This enlarged my acquaintance, others came with me, and I held preaching services from the Don Bridge to Queen's Park. Some who had heard me on the north of Yonge St. thought I would do better if I had a hall, and desired me to see what the cost would be. So I enquired the cost of the Shaftsbury Hall which was $25.00 a night, the Agricultural Hall $20.00. The old Covenanter's Meeting house could be had at $9.00. But after all my efforts, I found no sincerity of purpose towards me in the man who proposed the undertaking.

1875. In May, 1875, I arranged to go to the township of McMurrick, in Muskoka, into the proposed temperance colony, and there did some carpentering about a saw mill which was being erected. There were then but two shanties in the township, the one belonging to the mill, and another on the edge of Doe lake. It was said of McMichael who lived there that he carried the first bag of seed potatoes to plant, 15 miles through the bush on his back; but that is but a small matter in pioneer bush life. We did not see fresh meat, except deer meat, till the following Christmas, when a settler killed an ox.

In passing in to the mill I was encouraged by the hospitality displayed. From Rosseau we had a walk of 30 miles, passing through a Scandinavian settlement. The first we met was a Dane, who gave us kindly advice, telling us that we could not get to the mill that night, and directing us where to halt. It was about 6 o'clock when we arrived at the door of the man with whom he directed us to stay, who proved to be a good man as we had been informed. He also was a Dane. When I enquired if we could shelter there for the night, the good man and his wife welcomed us in, and quickly set a meal before us. There were six in our company besides an eight months old baby girl. I do not know the number in the family of the Dane, but the family was large. They put us into their beds, and went without themselves. When I came to pay the good man for his entertainment, out of our slender means, wishing to be as liberal as my means allowed, he returned me part of the money not taking more than the cost of what we had used. I found that they had their Danish Bible and I visited them monthly for prayer and exhortation. Most of the settlement came to these meetings—Swedes, Norwegians and Danes. I afterwards made application for them for a school, and later they wished me to take the position of school teacher. The first Sunday I held religious services in the bush, under the shade of the green trees, our seats being the logs. There may have been in all about twenty present, nearly all intending settlers. For fifty Sundays I held services once or twice a day. Some from the Ryerson settlement joined with us. I also held a Sunday afternoon or evening service there.

When fall came on I was advised to locate in Ryerson for the winter, so as to obtain milk for the infant. It was a four miles walk to the mill.

1876. I held services in Monteith, Ryerson, Perry and McMurrick townships, and after a year concluded that it would be better for me to remove to a more settled part, so I took my family to the town of Parry Sound, June 1876, remained there eighteen months, working at sundry jobs, as carpentering, waggon making and furniture making, for some time, holding daily services. I commenced by holding Sunday services in the court house, then in the school house, temperance hall and the highway. But finally I was left where I began. No man would know me so as to furnish me with necessary means to meet any cost. The honest toil of the poor whether in Christ's cause or in the ordinary labor of life is but little esteemed, but in the day when Christ shall judge the world in righteousness things will be different.

In one of the books I have had for sale, in the good work pursued by the Mission, was a tale concerning a stone cracker in a rural district in England. He was about to have his dinner, sitting on a heap of stones, his fare being of a humble kind, but he gave thanks to God for it in plain words. The Esquire who owned the adjoining lands, was looking over the hedge, and hearing the poor man's grateful acknowledgments of his Maker's mercies to him, ridiculed his offering of thanks for such a meal, saying he should want something better than that to give thanks for, and went his way. Some time after the Esquire had a dream that the richest man in the county was going to die that night, so he began to think who was the richest man, and according to his reckoning there was none as rich as himself; so he concluded that he was appointed to death. He became excited and sent for the doctor, saying that he concluded that something must be wrong with him, for he knew that he had but little time to live, and the doctor was ordered to do what he could to help him. He went to bed, thinking he was not going to rise again. The doctor told him that there was nothing the matter with him; but the Esquire was convinced to the contrary, so he lay in bed all day and all night. He ventured to rise the following morning and take a walk in his grounds, when the gardener came to him, and lifting his hat, asked him if he had heard the news. The Esquire asked, What news? and the gardener told him that John, the stone cracker, had died the preceding day or night. Then said the Esquire, That was my dream; I, with all my lands, thought I was the richest man in the county, but now I see that the stonecracker with his contentment and godliness was richer than I. God hath chosen the poor of this world, rich in faith and heirs of the kingdom which He hath promised to them that love Him. This became the means of the Esquire's conversion, showing that God uses what means He pleases to accomplish His purposes.

Some may ask if any good resulted from such services. I must just answer by God's Word, that it was at His word the labor was done, and He has said, He that honoreth me I will honor, and, Blessed are ye that sow beside all waters, that send forth thither the feet of the ox and the ass (treading in that which is sown.) We can afford to let God be true and every man a liar—for men of high degree are vanity and men of low degree a lie.

I had not been in Parry Sound many weeks when I was asked to conduct services nine miles out, which I did, sometimes every Sunday and sometimes every other Sunday. I continued to do so for more than twelve months. At Parry Harbour the tavern-keeper lent me his sample room, and furnished fire and light free of charge. I had intended building a hall there for union services, but that fell through. Our services in the tavern sample room will never be forgotten. These I think were the first public religious services held in Parry Harbour, except the open-air services and the mill boarding-house services which I had previously held there.

On one or two occasions I went to the school house fifteen miles east of Parry Sound, where the services were largely of a social character; such the Scripture declares they should be, though men have perverted it into literary, artistic, scholastic exhibitions, and many make merchandise of it; in many cases men do not mean to, but that does not alter the fact, habit has become second nature and the people love to have it so by reason of custom and perverted understanding, and instead of having godly fellowship, it is creature array. Going from the carpenter bench, like Christ, and the fishing tackle, like Peter, James and John, to get the anointing of the Holy Spirit, for the work of the Lord, is to them out of date. They get machine-made men from 16 to 20, who too frequently strut around with a black cane for a shepherd's staff, filled with clerical dignity less the power of the Holy Spirit to work regeneration in the heart, and lacking capacity to teach people to be conformed to the likeness of Jesus Christ.

At one of the meetings held at the fifteen-mile school house, the school teacher led in prayer, and for myself he earnestly prayed, Lord, let Thy servant's last days be his best days, let them have the glory of the setting sun. It was worth a great deal of labor to obtain such a commendation, and I doubt not this and many other such supplications are on their way to complete fulfilment.

1877. In October, 1877, I left Parry Sound to try to find some enlarged opening for Christian work, or means to carry out my evangelistic desires.

During these sixteen months in Parry Sound there were many evidences in that locality, of the brevity of life. The first month of my being in the neighborhood, entering a house ten miles out to get something to eat, I saw a woman whom I thought insane, except that an open Bible told me I was mistaken. At last she spoke and said, I have lost three daughters in three months; two were drowned and one died a little before. I asked her if she could say with Job, "The Lord gave and the Lord hath taken away; blessed be the name of the Lord." She said she could, but she felt it very sore. Many years after I entered the same house and still sorrow continued there; another daughter had died and a son had been shot. "Man is born unto trouble as the sparks fly upward." Later there was another accident in the district; a man was chopping and a tree fell on him and he was taken home to die. It was near the nine-mile school house where I held Sunday School and religious services. He had been a great backslider. These were his own words, and if he had died when the tree fell on him he would be in hell, but he died some time after, desiring to be with Christ which is far better.

The next I remember was a young man I had pressed to come to an evening prayer service at the six-mile school house, but he refused, and a few days later he was killed while chopping wood in the bush.

The next was a young man working near the six-mile school house. He died in a few days from a blow by a logging chain.

The next was a man and his son near by. The boy had fallen out of the father's boat. The father, being a good swimmer, plunged in and carried the boy to the bank of the lake, and returned for his daughter in the boat, and sank before he reached the boat, and the boy also rolled into the water and was drowned.

Another was a man and his three children, carried away in a very short time with diphtheria. In another house two children in the same way.

The last Sunday night before leaving I spoke in the open air. Among those listening was a lad; a night or so after, he lay dead in the bush. I went out of the house and saw the gaping wound in his chest, where the gun charge had entered.

The following winter the Wabanno steamboat went to the bottom of the lake with all on board.

These are undeniable evidences to us that we should be ready when the Master calls, to answer, Here am I, and to be at peace with God through our Lord Jesus Christ who has borne our sin and carried our sorrow, and by whose stripes we are

Religious services in the woods. (See page 61.)

1)

healed. As I went to Collingwood to seek some means, I knew not how, to carry on God's work, the father of the dead boy was on board. I held a religious service in the cabin, it being Sunday. So disconsolate was the father that he told me he would be glad if someone would shoot him, too, that he might be out of his misery.

There are lonely hearts to cherish as the days are going by. Oh the good we all may do as the days are going by!

I got to Collingwood but I knew not how to start my work. The town hall would cost five dollars. The Baptist preacher, as heartless as a stone, advised me to get out of town as soon as I got in. A colored man offered me his house for a prayer service, but I do not know that I accepted it. I did not hold open air services; perhaps I was weary. However, there was no opening suitable that I could find in Collingwood. I had my tools and looked in vain for a carpenter job. One of the saw mills in Midland had been burnt down just before. I was advised to go there, so I went; but no work was to be had. I filled in my time at waggon work, waiting to return to Parry Sound, but no boat came. I received a dollar and my board for my work, and I intended to walk back. I went to Waubashene by boat; and there I found employment at carpentering, and I sent for my family. There was a meeting house there but only one service a day, so I obtained permission to use the meeting house, and for many months held one service a day.

While in Midland I held one or two services. There was one meeting house there, used by Baptist, Presbyterian, and Methodist, and an English church. I occasionally went from Waubashene and returned in the evening. There and back was a walk of about 25 miles, but 20 or 30 miles of a walk was no trouble to me at that time.

About Christmas I went to work at carpentering on the Midland railroad at Oldfort, this gave me opportunity to hold religious services among railroad men. I was somewhat in my element, having at different times worked at railway work. About 300 men or more were working along the road between Waubashene and Oldfort. Several shanties being in the immediate neighborhood, on Sunday I endeavored to hold religious services in the larger one where I stayed, but the owner of the place said, I would like it well myself, but there is a rough crowd here, and I think it would cause trouble. I think, said he, the owner of the next shanty would let you have his place, for he has a different class of men. I went to the second shanty and received a kind and ready consent, and the meetings were held and numerously attended.

In the religious services that I have conducted I have endeavored distinctly to maintain these various features which belong to all pure and profitable form of religious services: First, praise and thanksgiving, prayer and supplication to Almighty God, in the name of our Lord Jesus Christ, the reading of the Holy Scripture with exposition of it, and exhortation by it, as well as the proclamation of the Gospel, and I fully believe that all true social worship must be inspired by the Holy Spirit, and is equally the privilege of every true believer in Jesus Christ, and while all things should be done decently and in order, it must be a heavenly home and family fellowship to be acceptable in God's sight, and the ministerial capacity implies character and work, rather than office and profession; as Paul says, "Though I speak with the tongues of men and of angels and have not charity (love, or the grace of our Lord Jesus Christ), I am nothing, and though I have the gift of prophecy and understand all mystery and all knowledge, and though I have all faith so that I could remove mountains and have not charity I am nothing." I fear that a great deal of the religiousness of our day is but an artificial get-up of sentimentality and display, lacking the Spirit's control, direction, and power, and therefore is ineffectual for regeneration. The sounding brass and tinkling symbol can be made to work charmingly, but it is without divine glory, power or life; dead, yes some of it twice dead, if without the Holy Spirit's presence Ichabod its name, (the glory departed.)

The religious services at Oldfort very soon drew forth the enmity of those who had no love for such exercises. The first evidence of this to me was that I was taken by the throat and gently shaken, which indicated tempest in the air. I took no notice, but went to my dinner, when I was assailed with outrageous profanity, in the hearing of women and children, with no one to call them to order; so I had to deliver my soul, by telling them lustily that they should be thrown out of any decent society. Upon this they got furious and clutched the knives, intending mischief, when others interfered. I reasoned with them and thought the devil had left them, but I was mistaken, for when I came in at night it was worse than before. So I quickly concluded that that company would not do for me, and went to the shanty where the meetings were held, and asked the people if they could give me lodging, which they readily consented to do, and because the foreman with whom I worked would not side with the rioters he had to leave at midnight, and had to turn in with myself. Though a Roman Catholic he attended the services and was well pleased to have been there.

Some time later the man of the first shanty came to me and said, You will have to do something to stop the trouble or we will have murder here. I said, You should be man enough to keep your own house in order. He said, We should have gotten along all right were it not for your preaching; you started the trouble, and now you will have to stop it before it goes too far. I asked him what he wished me to do. He answered, Get out a warrant; to which I said that I had no money to spend on him. He said he would find the money if I would get out the warrant. I said, If you wish me to do it I will do so.

The nearest magistrate was at Midland City, several miles distant; I got ready to go forthwith. He said, Take care of yourself; there are three men in the bush, and if you get into their hands you will not get out whole. I picked up my nail hammer and put it in my pocket, and I said, If they meddle with me they will get more than they want. He said, There is a house at the bridge at the end of the first wood, and you had better ask the man to go with you (his name I have forgotten), for if you meet the men you are sure of trouble. I related the circumstances to the man of the house at the bridge and he volunteered to accompany me. His wife was excited and offered him a revolver. He said, We will not take it, we will do without. So we marched away across the stream into the next wood.

We had not gone far into the wood when we met the three dangerous characters who immediately commenced to bully and threaten what great things they would do. My companion said in pretty plain terms that if it was fighting they meant he would thrash the three of them in very short order, and they need only begin to get it. He advised them to walk on and say nothing. They, thinking discretion the better part of valour, took their champion and went their way and we went ours.

We passed the time occupied in getting to Midland, in relating incidents. My companion told me of a bully blacksmith who lived near a village Methodist meeting-house, and was the terror of all the men who crossed his place wishing to go there. Finally there came into the neighborhood a Methodist preacher who determined to settle the matter. He announced his intention to hold a meeting at the meeting-house. The blacksmith awaited his coming, and informed him that he could hold no meeting there. The preacher told him that he was not capable of preventing him. The blacksmith replied that he would get thrashed before he got there. The preacher told him he would give him the opportunity of doing so, and took off his coat. The blacksmith was soon on the ground, roaring by reason of the pounding he was getting from the preacher. Finally the blacksmith consented to allow the preacher to go to the meeting unhindered if he would cease his pounding; but the preacher would only cease on condition that he would accompany him to the meeting-house and attend the service. There was no other way out of the trouble, so he consented, and this resulted in his conversion, and the peace of the neighborhood. Perhaps to the reader this may be no new tale. The whip of small cords was used in the temple and whether that was the origin of the cat-o-nine-tails or not, a taste of the same now and then by the lawless and profane, may serve as a wholesome lesson.

When we arrived at Midland City, which at that time was a small place with a big name, no magistrate could be found, so we marched to the little village of Wyebridge, a distance of four miles, where we obtained the magistrate's warrant, a constable to serve it, and a volunteer corps to enforce it, if necessary We returned to the scene of operation, but tidings of our approach had reached there before us, and the disorderly characters dropped their tools, picks and shovels, and took the shortest way out of their danger, going across the ice which cracked under their feet to the danger of their lives. They left a tale of lamentation that they had lost their work and had to take a long tramp.

After this there was no more grievous strife; any so disposed being quickly brought to order. Some were told that they knew nothing, and it would be better for them to say nothing. If they wanted to debate they were to debate with other men and not with me.

1878. Some time later there was a strike on the road, some of the men not having received their pay for many months. About three hundred took possession of the engine and the flat cars to go to Port Hope, a distance of over one hundred miles. They asked me to go with them. Their manner had become so considerate after the departure of the rowdies that I could not refuse to accompany them. They telegraphed the Mayor of the town—the late Mr.Craig—and the counsellors who provided for our reception at the various hotels at Port Hope. I had provided myself with some large posters for religious services, and obtained the use of one of the rooms of the Young Men's Christian Association for mid-day prayer and gospel service. I also held other meetings in the open air. The meetings were well attended; among the number was the good man, the late Joseph Scriven, the reputed author of the well known and beautiful hymn, "What a friend we have in Jesus." He prayed on behalf of the president of the Midland railway, Mr. Hugal, with remarkable emphasis. These were his words, "Oh Lord, turn Thou the heart of that wicked man Hugal." As this expression will indicate he was a remarkably sincere and godly man and his life told marvellously for good in the town and neighborhood, as the residents well know.

Our friend Scriven was somewhat peculiar, as the following incident will indicate: When leaving the town and bidding him farewell he handed me a dollar, saying, "Your wife may have need of this, but I do not give it on your behalf." There are not many men possessed of a character like unto his. Since then I have had many profitable communications with him. I pressed him earnestly to take part with me in the mission work now pursued. His last expression concerning it to me was, The Lord provide you someone else, but I will not go. On my next enquiry the following year I learned he had been drowned.

I had a permit to hold services in the town hall, which I did, but after much contention with the man in charge, though having the Mayor's permit. We remained twelve days. The men's wages were paid only after they stopped the trains from travelling, which they did for three days.

One remarkable experience there was, a big flood caused by heavy rains, breaking up ice, bursting the dam and overflowing the river. This was in March, 1878. It was a terrifying sight to see the mighty rush of waters, carrying away bridges of stone and wood, which indicated the power of the Most High.

When our wages were paid, and we were about to return, a remarkable incident occurred. One of the men entered the train, apparently well, and suddenly fell and was taken up dead. It was a grievous matter to remove him to a flat car on the siding and leave without him.

On their return the strikers were shut off from work on the

railroad, whether from the company's want of means, or as correction for insubordination, I know not, but at Waubaushene I was kindly treated from first to last.

I went through various parts of the neighborhood seeking work and conducting religious services. I had a Sunday School and held prayer services at Oldfort, visiting Coldwater, Victoria Harbour, Midland, Penetanguishene, Wyebridge, Barrie and other places, holding prayer and exhortary services, which gave me much labor and walking, and some danger from exposure to the cold, although I generally endeavored to be cautious and not undertake more than I could get through safely. To avoid being frozen I had to shelter one night at Oldfort. I was desired by a friend to conduct services at Victoria Harbour (or Hog Bay as it was then called), but I would not venture there because of rain and flood. At the time my friend was much vexed with me for not fulfilling my promise; but my good friend and his companion were afterwards drowned together by being unduly venturesome.

I soon found work upon the mill property, but the wages being low, and the work hard and somewhat unsatisfactory, I concluded to go to the United States, and find work at carriage building. I started for Port Hope intending to cross by boat to Rochester, N. Y. All the money I had to start on the journey was 20 cents and a little food, and a drizzling damp day to begin with. I made twenty miles to Orillia about noon, and met a preacher of the town with whom I formerly had kindly social intercourse, as far as my means would permit, but now that I was away from home and without employment, he favored me with some cheap exhortation upon discretion and good conduct, to which I meekly said that my trust and hope was in God, which he had sense enough to admit was good to do; but he had neither hospitality nor natural feeling enough to say, Come home (which was a few steps), and take something to refresh you before you go farther this disagreeable day.

So I marched on through the rain (which went in at my neck and out at my heels) till long after dark, when I struck a tavern beside the railroad. I entered and hailed the landlord to know if he had a spare bed I could have for the night. He said that he had, and I told him that I would be glad to stay. "Bad night to be travelling," said he, "let me help you off with your coat." So I thanked him and soon said, I would like to get off to rest. As he showed me the room I said that I wanted to pay him, but money was not plentiful, and I must ask him to draw it mild—meaning the price. So he said, It is hard times, I know, for workingmen, I'll charge you ten cents, which I was pleased to pay him as I had expected his price to be twenty-five cents. I rested well till the morning. My cash was then ten cents. I wanted five cents for postage and paper to write home, and I needed something for breakfast. I hailed the tavern-keeper, and asked him to give me five cents worth of bread. He said, Stay and get your breakfast. I commenced to tell him that I had only ten cents, and he said, That will do very well. I failed to write home for want of a stamp. I was pleased with the manner of the good man, although some would call him a bad one for keeping a tavern.

I went on in hope of finding work of some kind in the town beyond, but in vain. No one said, Are you hungry, or thirsty. I started again and weary, sat on the road ten miles from Lindsay. I began to think, what about the night, where I should lodge. I had a measure of confidence in God's care even in those circumstances and I concluded that when I arrived at the town the first man I saw looking at me was the one who would tell me where to lodge. So I came to the town and there stood a man with his back to the tavern wall. I hailed him, Neighbor, can you direct me where to lodge to-night, for I am a stranger here. He said, I guess you can stay where I stay. All right, I said, I will go. I said, Can you tell me where I can find a carpenter job in the town? You won't find that here, said he; I am a carpenter myself and am obliged to pile slabs in a saw-mill. On our way to the house, I said, I was thinking of going to Port Hope. Take my advice, said he, go no farther, for it is worse there than here.

By this time we got to the lodging house which proved to be his mother's. They were evidently farmers who had come to town to spend their last days, and were comfortable. As I had no cash in my pocket I soon proposed to go to rest, gave him my bundle, and promised to pay her on the morrow, but where the money was coming from I did not know. No dinner, no supper, no breakfast, save when I sat to rest ten miles from town, as I started to try to stagger along, I found an orange at my side, and said, The Lord knew my circumstances, so I thanked Him for it and was refreshed by it.

I searched the town for work and concluded that the best thing to do would be to go back; so I went to the Midland railway station master and told him that I had worked upon the road, but they had stopped the work so I had come there seeking work, and there being none, I asked him to pass me back to Waubaushene. He said he could not do it himself without the consent of the head office at Port Hope; so he advised me to go to the Mayor who would give me a pass.

I was simple enough to do as I was told. The Mayor said, They have been getting the money, and they should pass you back; and refused to give me a pass. I said, What am I to do, no money, no work and no favor, and my bed to pay for and no money to do it with? So the Mayor said, I will pay for your supper, bed and breakfast. I felt gratified that I could pay the woman as I had promised. In this you can see God's care.

I returned to the station to tell the result, but before I reached it he shouted, Here! I have a job for you. I said, What is it? Seventy cords of wood to cut. I asked the price to be paid. Thirty-five cents a cord, one cut, said he. So I closed the bargain at once. Immediately there came another man to say, I have got a man to cut your wood. Too late, said the man, I have just concluded the bargain with a man from Waubaushene who has worked on the road. The new comer was another sent in the providence of God to help me. He said, Have you a buck-saw. I said, No. He then asked me if I had a saw-horse. He sold me the buck-saw and lent me the saw-horse. I then went and paid the lodging, got my breakfast and returned for work. I was told to go to the carpenter shop and sharpen my saw. When I got there I was hailed by the carpenter inside, Hallo, how came you here? On my legs, I answered. But where have I met you? I heard you preaching in Port Hope. He must have been one of the company who went there for his pay at the time of the strike. From him and others around the yard I received remarkable kindness, but the utmost I could do was to cut three cords of wood a day; one dollar and five cents was little money to keep two homes. I had arranged to hold religious services on Sunday in a hall belonging to a tavern-keeper, who expressed himself as being well pleased to have his hall used for such a purpose.

I concluded that if I continued to work there my family must come down, so I asked a pass from the station master for them to come to Lindsay. He said that the agent of the road would be there in a few hours, and he would probably consent to it. When the agent came he said, Get on the train and go back to Waubaushene and go to work on the road. This ended the present experiences in Lindsay. In this we can see how the Lord controls the circumstances and provides the necessities of those who serve Him.

This dates at about April, 1878. I took my departure in a box car. My friend, the carpenter, was professedly an infidel. However the kindness of his heart led him to provide me with a couple of dollars as soon as he knew of my distress.

My arrival at Waubaushene was an agreeable surprise to all at home. The men on the road received me as kindly as we parted when we went to Port Hope. I had the privilege of working on the road, and if I found a better job I could take it and return to work on the road again.

I continued at Waubaushene till about July, and then said farewell to the many friends at Waubaushene, and sailed for Parry Sound. I have a pleasant remembrance of the Christian kindness shown me by the manager and the assistants at the mill, as well as others. I had made improvements on a lot of eighty acres which I designed to settle on. My right to sell the improvements having been disputed, the government gave judgment in my favor, so I concluded again to occupy it; but found my second attempt as perplexing as the first, and the improvements, which cost me one hundred dollars, on leaving Parry Sound in December, I disposed of for a barrel of flour.

Before leaving Parry Sound the Scandinavians of the township of Monteith, Muskoka, desired me to take charge of the school which some time before I had written to the department to have established among them. But I concluded that my work was Gospel preaching and not educational teaching, so I declined. The only opening for honest labor in Parry Sound at the time that I could find, was to go into the bush lumbering, for which they paid $12 a month. Of course the board was additional, and considering how far we could make the $12 go between my wife and six children, we concluded that under those circumstances some of us would have to be buried before spring. So I said in my heart, Farewell Canada, here goes for Britain, passing through the States.

A vessel for Detroit was being loaded with lumber at Parry Sound. I asked the captain if I could sail with him. He wished me not to take the journey by reason of the danger of sailing so late in the fall. He said, I would not go myself if I was not obliged to. So there was nothing for me to do but to take to the road, as the captain's papers did not permit him to take me as a passenger. The following year about that time .

the steamboat Wahbono sunk with all on board, showing the correctness of the captain's judgment.

I sold a little pig for $2 and left the money at home, with the barrel of flour, and started for the road as straight as I could go for Rochester, New York. I met one of the attendants at my preaching services at the nine mile school house, and we went into the bush and had prayer together. I reached the fifteen mile school house, where I had also held services, spent the night with a godly family, and went on my journey till the next night, and received the hospitality of a tavern-keeper, and the same the following night farther on the road. I continued to march along, accepting hospitality where I could find it and did not seek in vain.

The snow increased in depth as I travelled along, and in the dark I found it difficult to keep the beaten track, sometimes getting knee-deep into the snow, so I concluded to make an early stop. Providentially I found a man waiting for me on the cross road, so I asked him where I could find a lodging for the night. He said, You had better come in with me. Supper was ready, he and his sister invited me to take a share, and I concluded it right to give thanks unto the Lord, which they endorsed with, Amen. By this we began to understand each other. They said that their father had given a piece of their land for the building of the Methodist meeting-house. I could say like Abraham's servant, "The Lord brought me to the house of my Master's brethren." When they knew I was a carpenter they thought to retain me in the town to do some work for their school. I was requested to stay until Monday. Had the use of the Methodist meeting-house on Sunday morning for divine service. In the usual manner the plate was passed around for the collection which amounted, I think, to twenty-eight cents, twenty-five of which I dispatched to Parry Sound, and three for a postage stamp. It is a small matter to relate, but it will indicate the life of an itinerant preacher. I shall ever have in pleasant remembrance the Christian hospitality shown to me by the good man and his sister. Their recompense must come from the Lord, for I have not found opportunity to discharge it.

I had, at this time, become seriously impressed that I must go to Toronto and tell of the need of Christian Workers in the district of Parry Sound and Muskoka, and see if any would help me to continue the work already begun. It was an inward prompting that I could not resist, much as I felt myself opposed to going to Toronto. I believe it was a Divine prompting though the results appeared at that time but little, as we shall show later.

Carpentering was a failure,so I said farewell,and went on my way. A good friend whose acquaintance I had previously made invited me to tarry for the night, but I concluded to go farther, I however failed to find a second welcome. The night was cold and the snow was deep but I was vexed to find I had sought in vain a shelter. On the road was a Methodist Church and from it drove a company of men. I shouted to them, "Any man in this neighborhood who could shelter a man for the night without money? They said,"You are in the right place. There is a man at the back of the lot who will receive you if you go to him." I said, "I have been through many such lots and am tired of refusals." They said, "Go in, you will be all right there." I asked, "Is he a Christian?" They answered, "He was a class leader with the Methodists." I said I would pay him a visit. I asked him if he would shelter a man for the night, who had no money. Peering out of the door he said, "I have much sympathy with suffering humanity, but you have come too late. I said if I went farther I would be later still. His answer was, "I have great sympathy with suffering humality but I can do nothing for you." I asked him if he professed to be a Christian. He opened the door a little wider and said, "Yes." I said, "If you close your door on me you will close it on your Master, mind." He meekly asked me to come in and be seated and, I will get you some supper. I said, I need no supper but to get shelter from the cold. He said, "If you would have come earlier I would have made you more comfortable." So he made me comfortable beside the stove for the night. There was brotherly kindness with him when he told me at the breakfast table not to be so late before I provided a place to stay for another night, should I need.

My next stage brought me to a waggon shop where I found a little work, and then arrived at Toronto. The larger portion of the earnings I sent to the family. My first work was, to go to the most competent man, according to my judgment and have a talk concerning evangelization or gospel preaching through Parry Sound and Muskoka, and relate to him my labours and experience and the condition of things during my three and a half years' sojourn there. I did so; to which the man said he was pleased to know my interest in the gospel but such was the condition of things that they could not keep the men paid that they had out at work, so my application could not be entertained; but while I continued in the town I would be welcome to attend the Sabbath or week day services, which I did, the following day being Sunday. I considered that so far I had done my duty, and as there was no response where I expected, and ought to have found it, I concluded that the best thing I could do was to seek employment at my trade, concluding I had cast the responsibility on another's shoulders, who should have been able to get help. Therefore in my simplicity my conscience felt at ease. I had not gone many steps when I fell into conversation with a man with a bar of iron on his back. I enquired of him the location of a man in my trade with whom I thought I might find employment, and he gave me the information I asked, and then asked, "Are you in that line? and when I said I was, he said, I am in the same line. You a wood worker and I a blacksmith, so I had to give him, in some measure, an account of where I was from, and how I had got over so much ground. He enquired how I was provided for the morrow, which was Sunday. He said I have not much in my pocket, but what I have got you shall have, and I wish you luck. I live on Young St. If you get a job come and see me, and if you don't get a job before you leave, come and see me. I could find no employment in Toronto.

On the day before Christmas I met the friend who had seen us off more than three years before when leaving for Muskoka. He was provided with a big turkey for his Christmas fare. He gave me an Irishman's welcome to his home to share his Christmas fare, and to remain.

After a week's ineffectual search for work his wife said, That minister that you have been to see is able to put in a word for you, so that you could find something to do, and he should do so. I am generally simple enough to do as I am told unless I can find a good reason for doing otherwise, and in attempting to fulfil the wish of others I often find that they are mistaken, and so it was in this case. However I presented myself on desire to the person on whom I had called about two weeks before. I said, Since I have seen you I have sought in vain for work. A friend of mine expressed the thought that you might interest yourself enough that by your influence an opening might be found for me. With an air of stiffness he said, Come in, and then said, Do you think I have nothing else to do but to hunt up work for men out of employ? Let the men who want work hunt it up for themselves. You came to me about gospel work, and now you come begging. If you had asked me for twenty-five cents in the first place I would have given it to you. I judge your profession of the gospel is cant and hypocrisy. I think that is about the roughest and most unceremonious address I have ever had from a man of culture. I said to him, If you were lying in the gutter outside and could not get up you would ask the first man that passed to help you. That is just how it is with me, but you have a fine house and think you are unapproachable. You have judged my profession to be cant and hypocrisy without evidence, and now sir I judge you by the evidence that you have shown that your profession is cant and hypocrisy, and that you are contemptible, and I abhor you.

I took myself away and resolved to withdraw from Toronto, and went forthwith to say farewell to my blacksmith friend on Yonge St. The Lord's thoughts are not men's thoughts. Immediately my blacksmith friend said, I am very sorry you could not find work. Had you been here this morning I would have gotten you a job cutting fire wood, handed me twenty-five cents and said, I hope you are not intemperate. He said there was one person I had not seen, and I must see him forthwith, and feeling myself a debtor for his kindness, I took his counsel and a change came upon the scene. I obtained employment at once which proved to be in the line of God's providence. I had not long worked until I had a severe attack of rheumatism which put me in an anxious and painful condition, during which time my employer very kindly attended to my necessities. Following the medical counsel, I went to the hospital with the purpose of laying up and obtaining proper treatment. At the sight of the premises of the hospital I lost courage to enter the gate, and as I had travelled to the hospital I concluded I would go to the place of work. I tumbled over the timber of which I was to make a waggon, and in the morning arose and went to work and lost my rheumatism. It may have been a dread of the hospital that helped to make the change, but a kind providence had ordered it. I soon attended the Baptist services in the town through the influence of my employer, and for a time had much pleasure in the association.

1879. About this time I commenced holding prayer services. This was in 1879. At seven in the morning I held meeting at the Queen's Park and also others during the day, and occasionally in the streets. About this time the Bible Society advertised for a lecturer in their work. I made application to represent them, but my application was declined. Before the close of the year severe attacks of fever assailed several of my family, causing the death of an infant.

1880. Early in the following year, which was 1880. I availed myself of an opening in my trade in Rochester, New York, designing to go to England. The previous sickness in my family prevented my taking an opportunity that presented itself. I soon commenced to hold street meetings in Rochester, which was something novel to them. One woman passing expressed her approval by lustily saying, Bless the Lord, brother, you are on the house top. I had the pleasure of making numerous acquaintances interested in the Lord's work. We joined together in social prayer and Christian confidence and kindly association, and soon we joined together for open-air service on Sunday afternoons. Our company was numerous, and the services interesting, but some who had no pleasure in the good things in the kingdom assailed us with a shower of rubbage, and the most of the little flock scattered. The only one that remained of the company was an Irish widow. The soldiers of the cross couldn't well stand the fire of the artillery of the prince of darkness, the lack of true grace being the cause. I was told that the adversaries came from one of the Roman Catholic churches, and recommended me to see their priest. On calling upon him he said he judged the Lord had not sent me to read His word to the people. There was no use in complaining to him. If I wanted redress I would have to go to the magistrate.

About this time a Baptist brother and myself arranged to work together in preaching the Gospel through the country, and circulating the Scriptures. We had to set a time to commence, and at the appointed time I told him I was ready for the work, but he deferred to start at the time, saying he would be ready shortly. But his time never came. He displayed an adverse spirit. I saw him a few years afterwards, a little time before his death. He was then sick in bed. He said, I have desired to see you more than any other person in the world. In answer to my enquiries to his condition he said, I am as though a thousand demons were tearing me to pieces. Some time later he escaped through the hospital window and jumped the railings of the bridge into the river and died shortly afterwards. He expressed himself before death to the effect that the Lord had chastened him by reason of his disobedience, but with his last breath he was heard calling upon the name of Jesus. The Lord said, If any draw back, my soul shall have no pleasure in him. But the apostle says, "We are not of them who draw back unto perdition, but of those who believe to the saving of the soul," and to this every true believer can heartily say, Amen!

I sought some encouragement and help of the Bible and Tract Society of Rochester, New York, but found no material help. At this time a message was sent to me by a Christian man stating that I could sell Bibles and scripture books for him on a commission, but it was not very encouraging.

With much labour and accomplishing but little, after a period of six weeks or two months I was offered work in a box factory, which I accepted. I continued to hold open air services, and to distribute tracts on Sundays, and in the fall I rented the old Quaker meeting house in Brownes square. I gave notices in the paper concerning the services to be held. Before opening the premises for the public, at the house of the aged Irish widow before mentioned, where we were accustomed to hold weekly prayer services, a good brother who had read the notice in the paper said, So far you have done right, but unless you call on the business people you will get no funds. So I started upon the line that he proposed, of calling on the business houses. A Christian medical man introduced me to a lumber man who furnished me with the material to make benches, and to fix the premises. Another gave me a chandelier. The man who gave me my counsel painted my sign, and I was provided with hymn books and cash donations.

When I started, those that I anticipated would have helped with me had started another meeting at the Quaker meeting house at the other end of the town. However these meetings were kept going for ten weeks. Finding it difficult to pay the last month's rent and not wishing to contract debts that I could not pay I asked the landlord to take possession of the benches, which he consented to do. Some young men who had attended the meeting, but who had been disorderly and thereby had caused discouragement, upon the closing of the premises, accompanied me part of the way home. They expressed their regret, one of them sincerely saying that that place would have saved some of them from jail, and perhaps some from the gallows.

1881. After this I held many meetings around the town which brought us into the year 1881. On several occasions the mayor permitted me to speak on the court house steps, and the police were there to keep order.

Finding no opportunity of returning to England, upon reflection, ¶I concluded that the United States was a good field for Christian work, there being a population of fifty million, while

Canada had only five million. But by this time I could not find any advantage in comparing the surroundings with that of Canada, so I resolved to return to the place whence I came.

One of my former fellow labourers in the gospel in Toronto had pressed me in coming over to tarry at his home. Upon arriving at his place I received a hearty welcome. I soon found employment, and among the operations was to fix up at the race course. My conscience seemed to say, This is poor occupation for a gospel preacher. My good friend with whom I stayed was accustomed to take a morning walk before breakfast, and on one of those occasions an adversary poured into his ear the poison of scandal, although the gentleman who did so was accustomed to give exhortations upon divine subjects. My friend on returning to his home, commenced an onslaught on me concerning what I ought to be and what I ought to do, in contrast with what I was doing. I said, You pressed me to abide at your house, and I accepted your invitation, but with no desire to be a burden to your bounty. You will please come with me to your wife and understand that I have arranged to pay for my expenses while here, which I had then discharged and told him that I judged he was unworthy of my company.

One of the things the Lord hates is the man who sows discord among brethren. I was very grieved to lose the fellowship of one whom I esteemed a Christian friend. This was the work of the mischief maker. At the close of the year he wrote me, after I had returned to Rochester, and asked me to forgive the wrong he had done me. I wrote him that I did freely forgive him, but I could not think of him as the wise man that I had formerly judged him to be.

After a few months one of our former Christian acquaintances called upon me in Rochester. I enquired of him concerning the person before spoken of. I learned that he was buried some time later. I saw his widow. I enquired the cause of his death. It was a grievous matter to speak of. She said he had gone out as usual in the morning and that was the last. I judged from her expression that he was brought home dead.

I had arranged to bring my family across, but the man to whom I had committed the matter blundered and occasioned a delay. During this time I ran a nail into my foot which disabled me from work. I had to return to Rochester an invalid. I again attempted to maintain a Christian work in Rochester,

A Woman who had a remarkable vision. (See page 34.)

sustaining myself by various operations, carriage work and carpentering, and finally became broken down in health and reckoned that if I tarried much longer I would have to be buried there as two of my little ones already had been.

I must relate a little incident which had occurred while there. In buying a newspaper one night from a blind man I said to him, Friend, has the Lord opened the eyes of your understanding to know Jesus? Is he your Saviour? and he shouted with gladness, "Bless the Lord, He has," that he could be heard across the street. After this we got intimate, and he was accustomed to spend his Sundays with me. There came to the town a man who said he could do miracles in giving sight to the blind, so I mentioned the matter to him. He said, It is true. I know some who couldn't see and he has been the means of giving them sight. I have been thinking that perhaps he could do something for me, he said. Wouldn't it be grand to see the fields, the flowers, and the birds? I will go and see if he can help me. The next Sunday he came as usual, and I said to him, Did you see the doctor? So he said rather mournfully, Yes. I asked, What did he say? He asked me if I ever could see, and I said, No. The doctor said, I can do nothing for you. The tears coursed down the big man's face as there was no hope for him. I have seen him since with Scripture passages on boards on his back and breast telling that the wages of sin is death, and the gift of God is eternal life through Jesus Christ our Lord. He has a tin cup to receive any gift that the godly or benevolently disposed may deposit there. My blind friend said there was a great deal of dissatisfaction about his carrying the cup. Some of the professors of religion who I judge are rightly termed cranks, would often say to him if he trusted in the Lord as he ought, he shouldn't carry that cup. While those persons are so ready to give their counsel, they are often not so ready to bear the burden, and do not remedy in themselves the faults which they suppose exist in others.

1882. Again in 1882 I found it necessary to leave Rochester, by reason of physical weakness, I suppose the result of overwork. Pulpit preaching is esteemed honorable and laborious, but the highway proclamation of the Gospel with the majority is a thing of naught, and those who undertake to do such work are considered capable of bearing their own burden. But God's thoughts are not men's thoughts. He says, "They that honor me I will honor, and those that despise me shall be lightly esteemed"; and so the end will prove.

I concluded I would endeavor to find an opening in the Northwest, the country being opened up by the construction of the C. P. R. A way was opened for me to go to Port Arthur, but I saw an advertisement for carpenters at Algoma Mills which was only half the distance from home, with better pay. I earnestly strove to get to the latter point, but having given my word to give answer by noon either to go or not to go I conscientiously had to go soon after the tick of the clock, and well it was that I did. At night I was on the way to Port Arthur, but meanwhile I found the man that I had sought in vain in the morning. He said, I will send you at once if you will go. The boat leaves to-night. I said, I would like to go, but I cannot break my word. He said, If you are not satisfied when you get to Port Arthur write to me, and I will tranship you.

I left by boat at night. We passed through heavy weather and troubled waters. On arriving at Sault Ste Marie we learned that the Algoma Mills boat on which I should have sailed, had I gone there, had sunk with a hundred persons on board and only two were saved. I had the worst passage across Lake Superior I had ever experienced. Had the vessel gone to the bottom it would have been a matter of indifference to me by reason of the extreme sea-sickness I experienced. I held religious services at various times on board. A number of other men were on board, also going there to work. One of the company was, very debative, though professedly religious. One of the men who was very intemperate and not very orderly said to our debative friend, You can shut up. We know the manner of man you are. Your tongue has told us. Speaking of myself he said, That is a good man, and we will stick to him. This same intemperate man got pitched off the cars and had to travel with his head tied up, but whenever he met me he always hailed me heartily as his friend. After some time I saw him straightened and trimmed. I said to him, I am pleased to see the improvement in you. He said he had been a fool long enough, and now had pitched intemperance altogether. I hope he kept his word and attained to the grace of God. I don't know that I have seen him since. I found my strength return at Port Arthur. I often worked day and night by reason of the great press of work in the construction of the railroad, and transportation of goods to the West.

I had a conscientious objection to working on Sunday. I attended the Methodist services and had a desire to attend their Bible class. I sat for some time at the door, expecting a greeting, and to be invited in. Certainly my appearance was not very attractive. Man looketh at appearances, but God looks at the heart. I lost patience waiting, and I thought they were a little short of the respect they should show to a stranger. I found another way to improve my time. I went to the corner of the front street and endeavored to wake them up to duty by an open air proclamation of the gospel which was somewhat novel to them. For one of the newspapers in another town reported that they were not privileged with a Salvation Army in barracks, but we have a strong lung street-preacher who holds forth every Sunday morning. Keep at it, Mr Buskin. Just so in Port Arthur. I kept going on Sundays only, as I was so much occupied with work during the week.

Later I went into the lumber camps in the Indian reserve and had permission to hold religious services in the camp. On arriving at the camp my Bible fell out of my bag and a man made it lustily known to the rest that there was a man in the camp with a Bible. This ends the year 1882.

1883. We soon had opposition in religious service in the lumber camp. A gang of Frenchmen produced a fiddle and played and sang a chant and then they played up a gig. Our services though informal, was acceptable and profitable to some, and the Frenchman, some months afterwards, on visiting their camp many miles away gave me a hospitable reception and bought such French books as I had, and desired more.

Leaving the lumber camp, I went thirty miles east of Port Arthur on the construction of the C.P.R. railway. My first work on arriving was to severely cut my instep with a sharp axe, which laid me up for two weeks, and gave me opportunity for reading an edition of Fox's Book of Martyrs, which one of the men had lent me.

The man who hailed me concerning the Bible, in the lumber camp was the one who helped me to the camp when my foot was cut. He made known to others that the preacher was in the camp, and arranged for my holding religious service in the camp on Sunday. There were in all several hundred men working. After two weeks I was told either to go to work or leave the camp, so I hobbled out, but I suffered for many months from the wound during my stay at the camp. I held services three times on Sundays, and they were usually well attended. On return to Port Arthur I proposed to a Methodist minister that the men working on the construction, which extended for ninety miles should be visited, and religious services conducted among them, and supply them with scriptures and hymn books, etc. The Methodist minister said, if I would go he would furnish me with French scripture as he had a stock and he would try to get me a grant from the Bible Society. I told him I would reflect upon it, and give him an answer a day or two later. I reflected upon it and concluded I could spare a couple of weeks to visit them. I received the gift of the French scriptures from the minister but had to pay for those from the Bible Society. I packed them up in a flour bag put them across my back and started.

The first meeting I held was seven miles east where there were forty men at work. I was well pleased at the respectful reception I received There had been a dynamite explosion on the work some time before, one of the men had been blown over the dereck 40 feet high and was not very seriously hurt, while one of the stones killed a man driving a team a quarter of a mile distant. How many and marvellous are God's dispensations to teach men their dependence upon Him. I endeavoured to visit all the camps as I went along. In some places there was a measure of contempt, and in other places respectfulness and thanks. I sold the Bibles and sent for more by the teams. At one of the camps after holding religious service the contractor said he thought I should have taken up a contribution. He had spoken with the men and they said they knew me, and said I did not do so. He said, The Priest comes here sometimes and he never goes away without ten dollars, and though I am not a religious man I think you are as much entitled to it as he, and in the future you will give us an occasional call and I promise you shall not go away with less than ten dollars. During the two weeks I probably received twenty-five dollars in all, unsolicited, twenty of it being from the camp where I got my foot cut at which there were many Roman Catholics. One of them afterwards said, You have given that man twenty dollars, but if you had spoken to us it should have been seventy. We do it for our priests and we would just as soon do it for you.

During my journey among the camps I had conceived the idea of establishing a permanent work among them. I said to one of the contractors, I think I can accomplish it and begin by raising two hundred dollars at Port Arthur. He said, And then come to me, and I will have ten dollars for you.

On our return to Port Arthur I immediately took the town hall for two evenings, having in view the formation of a mission among the men, the Methodist minister taking part with me and also others who confirmed the evidence of good resulting from the religious services already held among them. The addresses were accompanied with prayers. I also wrote to the public papers and then endeavoured to raise funds in the town for the object. The cost of the meetings and the printing and the time spent amounted to seventeen dollars, to meet which I received three dollars and a half. I went to Mr. Ross the manager of the construction and told him of the matter proposed. He said he would be pleased to help in any way that would be to the men's profit, and especially to keep them from intemperance. He said, the best thing would be to send to the Syndicate and see what they would do. I asked him how long before we would get a reply. He said, Not before three weeks. I asked if I could go to work until that time. He directed me to his nephew in order to do so, and I worked for five weeks waiting for a reply at which time I asked him if the answer had come. He said he had sent in the application with other matters of a similar character and there had been no answer to any of it, and he supposed there would be none. So I concluded that I would take my departure for home at the first opportunity not obtaining the practical response.

The month of May was advanced, and still Thunder Bay was covered with ice till the eighteenth day, when a big breeze had broken it, and before night had blown it all away. The last cattle in the town were killed for Sunday's dinner, and sold at thirty-five cents a pound. On Monday the Steamer "City of Owen Sound" came in and beef was sold at ten cents a pound.

I now arranged for my departure by the boat. I think it was the 24th of May she sailed. Before leaving the Contractor who had invited me to give his camp an occasional call and said I should not leave without receiving $10 called at the tavern where I stayed, and said to me, We have not seen you lately. We thought you would have given us a call. I told him I felt I had done all I was able to do, for I had my family to look after, and I did not wish to undertake more than I was able to get through with. I had endeavoured to raise money for the work and had failed. He said to me, If I had your gift I would go to work and the money would have to come. The counsel of this good man who did not profess to be religious has frequently recurred to my mind and stimulated me under circumstances of discouragement proceeding sometimes from professedly religious people.

Having failed at Port Arthur in my endeavor in the work of the gospel, I thought I would renew my efforts in the city of Rochester, New York. I did so without success. I then asked my wife whether it wouldn't be better for us to go to Canada again. We sailed by boat, leaving two of our daughters behind who preferred to stay. We sailed to Toronto, and some time later to Algoma Mills. Through the kindness of him who had befriended me when I came from Parry Sound, I was furnished with a hundred Bibles and Testaments in various languages, a hundred hymn books, and sundry religious tracts.

We arrived at our destination some time in the month of September, having an engagement for several months. On the first Sunday I got the use of the round house for religious services, then the only convenient place to gather in, there being neither meeting house nor school house in the place. The meetings were continued there on Sundays until the weather became too cold. I soon put up a shanty that accommodated us while tarrying there. Dissatisfaction soon showed itself between the manager and employes at carpentering, my son being discharged with others, which I concluded was an outrage, and for saying so I also was dismissed.

The weather being severe I was afraid to leave on account of my family, so I remained. I reckoned I lost by the breaking of the arrangement, four hundred and eighty dollars,

The scriptures and books were soon all supplied, and many were pleased to get them. They were supplied in Swedish Italian, French, and English, and probably other languages, but I have forgotten. I obtained another supply of Bibles and hymn books during my stay. I made a visit from Algoma Mills nearly to Sudbury holding religious services at various camps and sawmills.

While at Vermillian River I purposed to hold services, but the enmity and opposition was too strong. I was pleased at the presence of the English Church missionary, Mr. Gilmor, who conducted the service, and I enjoyed association with him. He conducted a very profitable service. I had started work for a contractor. Some of our men fell sick, and among them the foreman. We had been sleeping in tents in a marsh in November. The foreman said, If I stay here I will die, so I will have to leave. I said, If you leave I shall have to leave too, for I am not pleased with the company. Our gang returned to Algoma Mills. On the way we found a company of Italians with several sick ones, one having his brother on his back. Between them they carried him thirty-six miles and brought him into Algoma Mills, not knowing that he was dead.

Soon the work came to an end by reason of a strife between the Grand Trunk and C. P. R. Most of the workmen were dismissed and sent to various points. I also left, but engaged work at the Vermillian Bridge. Immediately after arriving there I made up my mind to hold religious services if possible. I found a better reception than on my first visit. They consented to have the place in order immediately after supper. Notice was given and the bell was rung and the place was filled. The address was from the words in Genesis, "I am thy shield and thy exceeding great reward;" and another portion, "Walk before me and be ye perfect." I gave them, to the best of my ability a rousing exhortation, and I heard them afterwards say that it was very good—a very marked contrast to my former visit. On leaving a few days after they presented me with a voluntary gift of thirty dollars. I told them I was not working for money and I did not desire their gift, but I felt gratified with the evidence of interest, and said I knew there was a need of such work being done and I would put the money to the cost of going to Toronto, and endeavour to establish a permanent work.

1884. I left on the first of March 1884 and arrived in Toronto after a journey of three days and nights. I visited a friend in whose home prayer service had been conducted and on leaving in the fall with my supply of scripture and books I was heartily commended by prayer to the Lord. A Presbyterian minister usually attended them. On occasion of my leaving he gave an address and in some measure in speaking of myself, seemed to speak prophetically. He said, My father immigrated to this country long ago to seek a fortune, and with my father came a friend who came out to spend one. He said (concerning myself), my friend puts me in mind of my father's friend. He is rich in faith and he is going to the wilderness to spend it. I had not anticipated returning on the errand that I had come to Toronto for. The Lord who sees what is in the darkness as well as what is in the light is preparing the way for his work. My Toronto friend said, You have come at a good time. I am going to our class meeting to-night, I will introduce you to the leader and our rich brother there, and no doubt they will respond to your proposition. The latter had through my friend's influence, promised to furnish me with all the scriptures I wished to take, but having at the time all I judged I needed, I thankfully declined his kind offer. After the service I told them the result of my journey, and my errand in coming to Toronto. They were very genial and highly gratified, and were profuse in promises. The class leader requested me to call on him, as his time then was rather occupied. On doing so he reminded me that there were so many deceivers about that it would be well to have reliable evidence and then there would be no difficulty. I had with me the signatures of the men who made up the thirty dollars which I had nothing to do in obtaining beyond the exhortation. Yet, that was not esteemed evidence so I told him I would write and get the evidences into my possession which would confirm all that I had stated. I suppose it took nearly two weeks for the documents to come to Toronto. I thought I had in him a friend, and when I presented him the documents he still heaped upon them mistrust. I was so vexed with his insinuations that I felt I would fly to get from him. I could not have believed it possible that people who make such charming professions could practise such vile, heartless conduct as I had to experience. These may seem somewhat strong expressions but not more so than they merit. From neither of these persons have I received ten cents.

These experiences are records of facts, and not being quite a cast iron character the little sensitiveness had to smart under the unnecessary insinuation of evil that was attributed to me. I came to do work and not to go whining around.

I attended prayer services daily, asking the Lord's guidance and help, and the prayer of those present who were zealously affected in the good cause of the Lord, and many were the prayers, and many have been the answers, and many have rejoiced in the results. To one at the prayer service I said, I would like to get a hall where I could hold a public meeting. He said, I will take you where you can obtain one. I know they hold meetings there. I followed his counsel, but only to be grievously disappointed. Although I was willing to pay the hire of the room, I was probed with a variety of ungenerous and unbusiness-like enquiries which seemed to say, Without our permit you need not attempt your errand, and I left him in strong heat of contempt.

On the following day the same young man introduced me

to another person to whom I told my errand to Toronto. He said he would send me to the right man to put me through. He said he would be holding a prayer service at the west end of the town, so I danced away in full anticipation that the work was accomplished. I found the man I was directed to, and after greeting him made known my errand, and in a sulky manner he said, Oh, you are the man who was in our store yesterday. I asked, What store was that? On Yonge Street? So I asked him if he was the man I was speaking with. He said he was. I told him I left his store very much grieved by his expressions, thinking that a gentle reproof would be helpful to him. But he very plausibly told me that it did people good to be grieved sometimes. I found that words were not of much avail with him, so I thought he should understand my estimate of his character. I said I had come two miles for the benefit of the prayers of the meeting, but I judged his prayers were not worth waiting for. I occasionally met him while around the town. He appeared with a smile to be a little genial, but I had no confidence in his good will. Strange to say, his days were few. He died shortly afterwards.

I will not weary the reader with multiplying statements of the disagreeable disappointments in men and associations to whom I had looked for better things. Suffice it to say, I sought in vain, or almost so, all the Christian organizations in Toronto, but if my own hands hadn't been sufficient for me I would likely have been lying among the dead men, but all that has resulted I owe to the kindness of the Lord, and to Him alone I ascribe the praise, not being unmindful of individual sympathy. Finding everything a failure I put the following notice in the Telegram, February 10th, 1884, for which I paid sixty cents out of my last dollar:

A Gospel Mission has been commenced in Algoma district among Canadian Pacific Railroad men to circulate the Holy Scriptures, religious tracts, and minister the Word of Life, the base now at Algoma Mills. $700 is necessary for the year's expenses. Contributions will be solicited through the city for the same and reported by Geo. Buskin, Missionary. Communications addressed 12 Queen St., west.

This served to waken some up a little, for I was told the Religious Tract Society would take it up, and I should be sent out immediately. Upon delivering the message to their secretary they said it would be impossible to do so in less than a week. I said it was useless to talk about a week's time. My money was all gone and something must be done at once if they were going to do it. He said, Well, you can make out for the week and we will advance you a month's pay—forty dollars.

As I usually am, I was simple enough to do as I was told, —not thinking that Christian men made promises to break them and provided my daily bread by pledging my tools, and when I came to redeem them, they put exorbitant interest on them. I said to the man, This is murder. Murder? said the man, I would not like to do that. I said, That is just what you are doing; you are taking the bread from the children's mouths and the clothes from their backs.

At the end of the week the secretary of the Tract Society neither furnished me with the forty dollars, nor the material, or even ten cents to cover the cost of my time, but said they were not in a position to take up new work for they could not sustain what they had in hand, but if I was willing to do what I could, they would help me. This was a little light in the darkness, although at no time has their help been more than credit for goods, at 20 or 30 per cent. discount, all of which accounts to date have been paid. There has been a donation of a few thousand tracts in various languages during this time.

With this promise of help, I made another effort and wrote five letters to the various newspapers concerning my errand to Toronto, but the sum asked of me for its insertion in each case was five dollars. Finally the editor of the Globe said if I had someone to certify the correctness of my statement they would insert it. So I started to find one, and met one on the street and said to him, Will you certify my statements at the Globe office? You have known me longer than anyone else in Toronto, and you know what I have been doing up the lakes. They will insert my letter if they have some one to confirm the truth of it. He said, I would do it in a minute, but you know my circumstances. They would say to me, You have enough to do to look after your own work, and there would be trouble.

I concluded I had done all there was in my power, and as there was an advertisement for carpenters I arranged to go to work at Owen Sound. My three weeks'labour in Toronto brought only $2.10 till the 24th of March. As I was about to leave by train two letters were handed me; one saying he had read my letter in the Globe and he believed he was acquainted with my friends, and to call at his office. The other was from the Toronto News office, and stated that they wished to see me. Calling at the News office they handed me a letter sent to them for me from Cobourg, Ont., saying, " I have read your letter in the News of your proposed Christian work among railway men. My father is a railway man. I enclose you a small contribution and wish you God's blessing." I then went to the other office as directed and was kindly received, found he was acquainted with a cousin of mine of the same name. He gave me counsel and assured me if I acted upon it the work would start. He also sent me to his mother who gave me a contribution.

I was not aware that my letters had been inserted in the papers. The person whom I asked to certify my statement at the Globe office told me he had afterwards gone in and told them it was all right. In this you may see how a person may help or hinder a good cause by a little word.

March 22nd, 1884.

"Mr. Geo. Buskin is in the city for the purpose of obtaining means to carry on the Gospel Mission to the men employed on the Canadian Pacific Railway. For some time past Mr. Buskin has carried on the work of disseminating the Gospel among the labourers engaged on the construction work along the line of the Canadian Pacific Railroad in Algoma district, and also among the lumbermen working in the same section, since September, 1882. Mr. Buskin has supplied them with about 175 Bibles and Testaments, and 150 hymn books at cost price, and distributed two or three thousand religious tracts and small books, and held amongst them more than a hundred religious services in different parts. He is now seeking from the older settlements that assistance in carrying on the work which he feels to be necessary in order that he may keep pace with the rapidly increasing demands of the field in which he has chosen to labour."

I had now got started and put the matter in the best form my judgement and circumstances permitted. I fell back upon those that I was least acquainted with who had promised me their help. The first gave me a dollar, the second said, It is little I can do, but one sheep will lead another, and he gave me two dollars. I then commenced the town in order. The next gave me fifty cents, and said, If he knew more about it he would just as soon give me five dollars. The five dollars has not come yet. I was somewhat surprised to find how genial many were upon whom I called, and who gave me their help in a small way. One good friend said, Is there no one who knows you in the city? I said the Bible Society and the Baptist Book Room knew what I had purchased from them: and what had been sent me to Algoma Mills. So he directed me to go and get them to certify the same. It reads as follows:

Upper Canada Bible Society, 102 Yonge St.
April, 1884.
To Messrs............ Officers in charge............
Depositary, John Young.

Gentlemen:—At Mr. Buskin's request I gladly certify that what little dealings we have had with him in the matter of purchase of Bibles on credit, and payment for the same has been very satisfactory and think him quite a trustworthy man. Yours truly,

JOHN YOUNG.

Standard Publishing Co. Limited.
Publishers of The Canadian Baptist. S. A. Dyke, Manager.

117 Yonge St. Toronto, Apr. 3, 1884.

Gentlemen:—I made the acquaintance of Mr. Buskin upwards of ten years ago in this city. That acquaintance was renewed last autumn when he purchased a number of Bibles for distribution among the Canadian Pacific Railway men at Algoma, and we subsequently received further orders from him from that place. I believe that he is sincere in his desire to do evangelistic work in that district and that he has qualification for it.

Yours very truly,
S. A. DYKE

Returning with it, he said, Now you are all right. This gentleman is a solicitor. He gave me his two dollars and his kindness has continued to the present. After this I fell back upon those I was personally acquainted with, and also received their help. At the end I had received eighty dollars from business men and forty dollars from private houses, including ladies. It was not much but it served to set things going. The money I invested to the utmost in scriptures and books which were open to the inspection of those who had contributed. As there were at this time seventeen thousand men working on the construction of the railroad, under those circumstances I reckoned a personal application to the syndicate the right thing to do to accomplish the work, but eighteen dollars was the beginning and the end of all that I received from them, and I had to pay my own travelling expenses. The entire amount I received on the way from Toronto to Montreal, calling at intermediate towns, was two hundred and forty dollars.

It is due to say that having got started I obtained more practical help from the editors of the daily newspapers than from almost any one else. On returning I acknowledged in the Globe the amount received and my commencement of operations. The following is the copy:

Toronto Globe, Monday, June 16, 1884.

Algoma Evangelical Mission.

The following communication has been received since the Globe statement of the work of the Algoma Evangelical and Scriptural Colportage Mission to Canadian Pacific Railroadmen and lumbermen on March 22nd: A dozen other newspapers have followed their example cheerfully, the result of which has been the collection of $270 cash and books to the present time, giving the evidence that the desired end will be accomplished of sustaining the religious work among the men. Toronto contributed in cash and books for sale $113.40, also books for distribution; Hamilton $22.90 and religious tracts; Port Hope $15.90, with a promise of books; Cobourg $3.75; Belleville $13.35; Kingston $15.35, and books; Brockville $8.50; Montreal $74.75; books $6.60. It is now proposed to visit the men in the neighborhood of Mishamacotton, about 10,000 on the railroad, and then on the eastern portion 6,000 men, besides the lumbermen. Trusting that it may be for comfort and profit for time and eternity, and that by the blessing of God that which is necessary to sustain it may be forthcoming. Communications addressed to Geo. Buskin, 12 Queen St. west, will be promptly acknowledged.

I went to Algoma Mills and then to Port Arthur going a hundred and fifty miles east along the road, visiting nearly all the camps. I soon sold out all my stock and sent for more, directing them to be sent to Algoma Mills, but as they were delayed in coming I went to Toronto to see the cause and found they had been sent to Port Arthur. I took my ticket for Port Arthur, to lay off at Algoma Mills, but the boat on which I had started did not put in there, and I was left at Little Current, on the Manitoulin Island, which inconvenienced and vexed me, for I had but ten cents in my pocket, but I had a stock of Bibles and Testaments, and I think I had the most remarkable sale there that I ever had. I sold from noon to night all round the town. Three copies I sold to one tavern keeper and his wife, and at night two steamboats came in and I made numerous sales among the passengers and crew, and finally arrived at Algoma Mills.

I fell in with a man going to Port Arthur. I found him godly disposed, and able and willing to work with me, so I arranged with him to pay him a dollar or a dollar and a quarter a day and all expenses, laborer's wages being at that time $2.00 per day less $5.00 per week for board. For many months my earnings had averaged from $15 to $18 per week at carpentering, and laboring work being paid extra for overtime. He did good work, and we got along satisfactorily, working around Fort William and Port Arthur, and then going to Ross Port, and also east of that point. I then endeavored to buy a boat to go round the coast for there was too much time lost waiting for steamboats, but the only thing to be had was an Indian bark canoe. My assistant was a military man, and told me he could handle a boat, so when I arrived with the canoe he marched down with military tread and in the same fashion boarded the canoe which rolled over with him and sent him sprawling into the water. It was a necessary and useful lesson for him which he stood in need of before we began our journey, for he was strong in himself, but wanting in caution.

Some time later we were out in a big storm in which there is one way for a canoe to ride safely, and that is by allowing the wave to strike a little on the side of the bow. They needed very great caution as the waves rose high. Finding our boat getting into the trough I shouted to him to be careful and see where we were going. His answer was, You are serving a good Master and He will take care of you. I thought it a poor patch for his negligence, but providentially we arrived safely at the place we were bound for. The men at the camp expressed wonder that we escaped drowning.

Here and near by I saw remarkable evidences of interest in the Scripture by men of many nationalities. Also at this place I met a former Christian friend, a contractor, who received us with true Christian hospitality, and our evening prayer and gospel service was profitable, and well attended.

After making many calls we arrived at Nepigon, in which neighborhood there was a large number of men employed. Mr. Rennison the missionary to the Indians at the English church, received us with true brotherly kindness.

This ended our canoeing as the railroad laid back from the Lake, and we took our journey to Port Arthur.

This was my third visit to Nepigon. On the way I stopped at the camp of the friend who the year before had promised me ten dollars if I got the work started. We were received very cordially, and held evening service there. There were around the camps, a number of men who professed infidel principles, and my assistant got unduly excited during the opposition, both outside and inside the camp. I felt that his untimely expressions might cause them to throw us out of the camp, which would not be desirable at that hour of the night, so far away from other dwellings. However no further trouble occurred.

We then had thirty-eight miles to Port Arthur in a broiling hot day, which we accomplished by five o'clock. On the way I said to my assistant, In the future in speaking with men of infidel principles and especially in the camp. moderate your expressions so as not to give unnecessary offence. He said his tongue was his own, and he was going to use it. I said that it might suit him, but it would not suit me. I told him that he had had his pay and I would have no further need of his service. That ended our intercourse. Otherwise I was well satisfied with the assistance he rendered.

After this I returned to Algoma Mills and visited various points among the mills of the Lake and then to the Manitoulin Island. I had remarkable sales at Little Current. I arrived at Owen Sound the end of October, having a debt of nearly four hundred dollars to pay. There were some small portions of supplies that had not been used. I had altogether supplied seventeen hundred copies of Scripture books in thirteen languages. I arrived at Toronto on the fifth of November. This must serve as a matter of fact evidence of doing useful work which would have been done more extensively had there been means on hand to meet the costs of doing it.

I was regarded by the creditors for the books with a measure of suspicion that I had contracted accounts that I was not going to pay. Certainly money came in very slowly to do it.

1885. I went west as far as London and returned again to Toronto on New Year's Day, 1885, and spent the time in trying to obtain means to pay the debts. I received two donations of a dollar each, one from a lady and another from a gentleman, and on the following day divided it among the creditors, a dollar each. I said to them, Take that as an earnest that you will get the rest. The consideration for the work that I had done was but small. It was somewhat a grief to give a dollar for the best of causes, but hundreds could go for frivolous matters. Having little hope of succeeding with the people, I thought I would try to move the Government. I asked a permit to put a notice concerning the work, in the sitting-room of the house of the Legislative Assembly. I put it in plain words where all who came in could see, which brought me a few fifty-cent pieces. Some proposed my putting a petition into the House to obtain a grant from the treasury. I said if it would be supported I would quickly put it in which some members said they would do; so the next work was to prepare the petition.

362 Yonge St., Toronto, Ont.,
February 25th, 1885.

To the Honorable Legislative Assembly of Ontario:

Petition on behalf of Algoma Gospel and Colportage Mission for Railway and Lumbermen and others in outlying parts of the same district.

GEO. BUSKIN, Missionary.

We, the undersigned, having knowledge that a large number of men are engaged in the above district, in the above and other useful occupations by which they are removed a great distance and for a long time together from the benefit of public Christian worship, there having been found also among

"We were out in a big storm." (See page 94.)

them (we are credibly informed)people speaking seventeen
different languages, and these people require Scriptures
and other religious help. There has been contributed in
Ontario during the last thirteen months more than $600
for the furtherance of the above mission work, many Bibles,
and much sound religious literature of an undenomination-
al character has been supplied, amounting to about 1,100
lbs. in weight, besides religious services. Believing it to
be a good work we respectfully ask the honorable House
to aid the same with a grant from the Treasury that it
may be the more effectually pursued,—engaging if it be
your pleasure to assist this much needed work, to supply
truthful and witnessed statements of its utility.—Signed,
B. J. HILL, 15-19 Temperance St.; JOHN FIRSTBROOK, 273
King Street, East; M. NASMITH, 16 Maitland Street;
WILLIAM DAVIS & Co., Beachill Street; THOMAS WEST,
197 Carlton Street; H.B. GORDON, 23 Scott St.
GEO. BUSKIN,
Algoma Railway and Lumbermen's Gospel
and Colportage Mission,
362 Yonge St., Toronto.

I then got the signatures of practical business and Christian
men. Finally I called upon one more prominent business man,
on whose good will I reckoned. In answer to my application he
said, My dear fellow, you are wasting valuable time. I know you can
get nothing from there for I have been in the House. I would
rather propose that those who value the work double their contributions. I received from him five dollars, and then I went
for the Premier to know what could be done as some said, Yes
and others said No, and then I had a knock down blow. I saw
nothing could be done. I then made a printed application to
every member in the house.

The only answer was a foul letter, which on showing it to
the editors of the public papers, I understood the Toronto News
inserted it. One friend asked me if any one could certify the
work I had done, and if someone could, to get a statement
from him. The following is the statement:

Trinity College, Dec. 10th, 1884.

I hereby certify that whilst doing missionary work along
the line of the C. P. Railway during the summer, I frequently

met Mr. Buskin who is engaged in holding services among the men and distributing tracts and Bibles, evidently doing a good Christian work.
E. A. OLIVER,
Divinity student.

Toronto, Dec. 10th, 1884.

During my visit to the North West last summer I had the pleasure of seeing Mr. Buskin. He was engaged in open-air preaching and Colportage work, and I believe was doing much good.
S. A. DYKE,
College St. Baptist Church.

I continued my effort to discharge accounts until I arrived at Montreal, when some public evil disposition was shown by a statement that the public was warned against me, and one of the company took away my collecting book and locked it up and refused to return it until compelled to by legal course, after which I was locked in an office and threatened with judgment of the law as a defrauder. But having the receipts of all moneys paid, and the amounts received, this device of mischief would not work. Afterwards there was an endeavor to prove that my statements were false. This they failed to prove. These matters occasioned several letters in the public papers. At this time there was a statement printed in the Montreal Witness, the date of which must have been April 27th, 1885, and reads as follows:

THE Y. M. C. A. WARNS THE PUBLIC.

To the Witness:—

Sir,—George Buskin is collecting funds in this city for mission work along the line of the Canadian Pacific Railway construction, and is using the name of the Young Men's Christian Association. He has no authority to do so, and I have written him asking its withdrawal. We have no knowledge of the merits of his work and have advised him to place himself in some society or committee of supervision.
D. A. BUDGE, Sec'y.

Some days previous to the statement of the Witness, the following had transpired between us:

Y.M.C.A., Victoria Square.

Mr. Geo. Buskin:—

Dear Sir,—When you asked of me the privilege of. letters addressed to our care, of course I only thought you referred to your private or personal letters. I could not think of you publishing us as receiving subscriptions, therefore you must withdraw it. You know my reasons: I have not confidence in your work. You should have some committee or society take up your work and support you in it.

Yours truly,
D. A. BUDGE.

REPLY.

Montreal, April 16th, 1885.

To Mr. Budge:—

Dear Sir,—I am in receipt of your note which shows so little of the charity which thinks no evil. I hope you will put it away before the Lord rebukes you, before your suspicious criticisms, consider the names and endorsations attached to my circulars. I will not say more than that I regret to find such anti-Christian conduct. Truly it can be said in the words of Jesus, "I was a stranger and ye took me not in."

Yours in Jesus Christ,
GEO. BUSKIN.

P. S.—You must remember the announcement of last spring in the Montreal Herald, May 24th, 1884. Algoma Gospel Mission, Geo. Buskin, Missionary; communications can be addressed to Y.M.C.A. for Mr. Buskin. My subscription book, which is forcibly and illegally retained by an ally of Mr. Budge, shows a contribution of about $850 in sums from 3c to $10 contributed in 38 towns, villages, etc., during 13 months. I have generally solicited my help from men of means from the Governor General and the heads of the government downward, including Bishops and the Clergy, not less than 200 persons. The money has been applied as follows: About 1800 books have been supplied in the Algoma District, including 500 copies of the Scriptures in 13 languages for which there has been paid, and I have received receipts for about $270. Personal travelling about $111. Printing about $46. Cartage of goods and purchases, $48. Paid for a co-worker in Lake Superior District, about $45. Then there is my own food and raiment, and that of my wife and children in the Algoma District. If any envy my field of labor let them go and do the work, for I have already announced to the Algoma District and the North West, for I intend, by God's help, to lengthen my cords and strengthen my stakes. I am especially thankful for help from many societies, not forgetting the Y.M.C.A. and Christians of all denominations, and hope that greater grace may be given to us all. My circulars have ten expression of confidence. It is for want of considering what is there that people are so rash. I wish to say that the Scriptures are sold at cost, and my books at Toronto prices, and sometimes less; and many thousands of tracts and magazines have been given away. Mr. Budge's colleague will please return my book and not waste my time and hinder a necessary work. I should express my thanks to the press for the support and kindness extended to me, and I believe the Witness will correct its mistake of the 30th of April under the head of correspondence."

To the attack upon me, printed in Witness, I was allowed the privilege of reply but not n the same columns.

The Montreal Herald of April 28th, 1885, inserted for me the following:

PROVE ALL THINGS.

To the Editor of the Herald:—

A statement appeared yesterday in the Daily Witness, headed "Y.M.C.A. warns the public," against Geo. Buskin collecting funds in the city for a mission work upon the line of the C. P. R. construction in the name of the Young Men's Christian Association which they do not approve, and he has been asked to withdraw. Having twice—first on the night of the 10th and on the day of the 11th, asked leave to use these words, or a similar expression in a printed notice, similar to that used before, "Communications can be addressed to Geo. Buskin, Missionary, at Y.M.C.A.," the statement that I am doing so in their name is a wilful blunder. The Editor of the Witness made his own statement of the work from my circular on the 10th inst., headed, "A good work," as follows: Mr. Geo. Buskin is working earnestly as a missionary among the navvies on the Canadian Pacific Railway; he has the endorsation of the Upper Canada Tract Society and of the Editor of the Canadian Baptist. This work ought surely to be taken up by the Y.M.C.A. or some other body. Subscriptions can be addressed to Mr. Buskin at the Y.M.C.A."

This statement was shown to Mr. Budge on the evening of the 11th, by myself, asking if anything in the direction stated could be done, and I was referred to Toronto. Nothing was then said of my using undue liberty, and small is the liberty if this cannot be granted, though I believe by God's help I can do His will and work without it. Mr. Budge's letter has already appeared.

Three notices appeared in succession. These statements are all given as they appeared in print. "To the Editor of the Herald, London House, G.T.R. Station, April 29th, 1885. I thank you for giving publicity to my letter in answer to Mr. Budge's statement in the Witness, headed "Y.M.C.A. Warns the Public," and beg to state that my collecting book has been returned through my solicitor, Mr. Crankshaw. I am, Yours truly, Geo. Buskin."

The following reached us from an independent source: Concerning Mr. Geo. Buskin. The following is an extract from a letter dated 25th inst., of Rev. E. W. Dodson, Toronto, Editor of Canadian Baptist, addressed to Rev. Thos. Henderson: "Mr. Geo. Buskin I have known since I have been in the city as a plodding worker in the cause of Christ. He is always received at Mr. Denovan's church with favor and his work highly recommended by the pastor." Mr. Denovan was formerly pastor of St. Catharine St. Baptist church in this city.

MR. B. VERSUS MR. B.

To the Editor of the Herald.

With reference to the correspondence in your good journal between Mr. Budge, Secretary of the Y.M.C.A. of this city, and the Missionary, Mr. Buskin. I hope with you that the former is not doing an injustice to the latter. However it does seem a strange proceeding, if correct, that Mr. Budge's colleague should take and keep in his possession the work belonging to Mr. Buskin. It looks as if there was a little jealousy peeping out of the matter, reminding one of a somewhat similar affair that occurred in Toronto a short time ago, and which caused considerable discussion in the convention of the Y.M.C.A. held in the town of Peterborough, Ontario, and which resulted unfavorable to the Secretary of the Toronto Y. M. C. A. (having since resigned) who was well known here as being connected with the Montreal Y.M C.A. I know nothing of the merits or demerits of this case, but as the Scotch idiot said to Dr. Guthrie, "Surely there is enough for us all to do."

Another statement appeared in the Herald at this time. About the day and date I am not certain, although it is marked April 30th. It is as follows:

MR. BUSKIN AND THE Y. M. C. A.

A private meeting of the officers of the Y. M. C. A. was

held yesterday afternoon when the difficulty existing between Mr. Budge, the secretary, and Mr. Buskin, was discussed. The conclusion arrived at was that the affair was merely a misunderstanding and Mr. P. S. Ross and Mr. Grafton were instructed to draw up a conciliatory agreement between Mr. Budge, the Witness, and Rev. Mr. Buskin. The member of the Y. M. C. A. who retained Mr. Buskin's subscription book has returned it to him, after being requested to do so by that gentleman's legal advisor. Mr. Buskin's address is, The Mechanic's Institute.

I afterwards learned from a friend now deceased, who knew the undercurrent of the trouble, that they had been made the cats-paw of certain vindictive persons in Toronto who I suppose thought themselves something like lords of God's heritage as far as they could make their dignity to prevail, and among them the man who I endeavored to instruct by telling him I regretted that I had wasted so much time and shoeleather upon him.

The mischief makers however, kept at work, and the following was inserted in the Montreal Witness, Saturday, May 9, 1885.

CREDENTIALS WITHDRAWN.

As Mr. Buskin's canvass has already gone beyond the extent contemplated by his friends, we deem it wise in the interest of the Christian public to withdraw our names from the certificate he uses until his work is placed upon a more satisfactory basis, and his accounts beyond question. F. A. McGregor, secretary U. C. Religious Tract Society. E. W. Dadson, Editor Canadian Baptist.

This last act I felt to be more grievous, disgraceful and injurious than the former, though I felt like fighting it, but my friends counselled me to let it die which I did as far as Montreal was concerned. When I arrived at Toronto I gave notice in the papers that I would hold a meeting in Queen's Park, and gave invitation to those who had started the opposition and accusations to face the matter with me and prove their statements, and none of them showed up.

Providentially I was enabled to go to work in Montreal at carpentering, though I had no tools, and earn enough money to meet my expenses and pay my fare back to Algoma Mills, a distance of more than 600 miles.

I was compelled under the pressure of the experiences

related to publish a financial report earlier than I had purposed, I had hoped when doing so to be able to say that all liabilities for supplies had been discharged, but there remained at this time about $80.00 to be paid to the Bible and Tract Societies and to the Baptist book room, both of Toronto.

Thinking it might be helpful to me, I received from the manager of the Baptist book room a note dated June 1st, 1886, 117 Yonge St. Toronto. This is to certify that Mr. G. Buskin has honorably discharged all his obligations to our company, and as far as I know from personal dealing with him he is worthy of confidence and support in his work as Missionary to the lumbermen and others. George Richardson.

My mind has been for a long time weighing over the subject of publishing the foregoing strife, but now thirteen years and a half later I am still subjected to the same blind, heartless, unchristian criticism from those who are at ease in Zion and certainly know better, but trusting in their creature resources and not in the living God.

The following is a report of my work at about this time:

REPORT.

At the request of friends in Montreal and with a view to meet the desires of all interested in the work, both in Toronto and elsewhere the following statement has been prepared as taken from my entries:

March 10, '84, to May, '85.

To paid railway and boat fares as per list....	$110 75
" printing........................	45 85
" carriage on goods and expenses in connection with the work...*..........	47 75
" rents of Town Halls for meetings, &c.	25 50
" Fred. Gilyatt, helper, as per voucher	34 30
" Missionary's salary, at $13.50 per week, till say 60 weeks to 4th of May	810 00
	$1074 15

CR.

By collections as per book:
Toronto.................$ 262 14
Montreal................ 156 21

```
Hamilton ..............    68 25
Kingston ..............    35 95
Port Hope..............    28 95
Belleville .............    22 55
Brockville.............    22 45
Ottawa ................    19 80
From 30 other places...   256 68
                          ───────
                                  872 98
```

```
          Balance................  $201 17
```
Montreal, May 4th, 1885.

The contributions have been from 1,300 persons and 15 public meetings, the largest sum received being $15.40 from a lecture upon Turkey, Palestine and Egypt, illustrated by magic lantern views, given in Toronto in aid of the mission by Mr. E. G. Lloyd, at the Lewis St. Baptist meeting house; also three other lectures were given but not as successful.

Contributions will be received and acknowledged with thanks by Mr. N. Macintosh, Mechanics' Institute, Montreal. Pending the formation of a Committee, the original account of expenses are with him for reference for those who have aided in the work. I providentially made Mr. Macintosh's acquaintance after speaking at one of the meetings for social prayer shortly before leaving Montreal at the first visit, and he became to me a kind, valuable and faithful friend and helper in the work until his death, which took place in 1894.

After I reached Algoma Mills, a then unknown friend from Montreal sent me ten dollars, of which I retained five for my necessities and sent five to my valued friend, now deceased, in Montreal, for Bibles.

Contributions and communications being slow I took work on the C.P.R. at Jack Fish Bay, Peninsular Harbor, and other points. I held religious services on Sunday. The stipendary Magistrate remarked at the time that the best way to have the Sabbath day observed was to keep the religious services going. I took what remained of my stock of scriptures and books with me, and made a number of sales. At this time the men worked Sunday and week days as well. The holding of Sunday religious services was not acceptable to all the company there, especially as I was now engaged in the mechanical work, so I soon had notice to leave, and fortunate for me too, as I discerned the untoward disposition of some of those I was among.

It was a slow journey getting from the place to Port Arthur. I provided myself with bread for the way, but I had a companion more hungry than myself, who also was going to Port Arthur to get his pay, so I shared out with him as well as I could and still he wanted more, but it was a hard job to get necessary food in that region. One person told me that he had to pay seventy-five cents for a meal of porridge. I got a little ungracious with my companion, lacking forbearance with his weakness. After arriving at Port Arthur my travelling companion hailed me lustily. He wanted to pay me the money and bread that he had from me. He was profuse in his thankfulness, and compelled me to lodge at the Hotel with him, which was kept by the man at whose shanty I held the first services on the Pacific Road. He said that he was delighted to see me, for he had heard that I was drowned while sailing in my canoe. I was equally pleased to see him on account of the generous manner in which he had opened his house for holding religious services.

I soon left by boat for Algoma Mills. When I reached there the five dollars sent to Montreal had brought back 100 Bibles and Testaments through the good offices of my now deceased friend. I was now enabled to go again to St. Joseph and Manitoulin Island. At St. Joseph I had a remarkable meeting with the Presbyterian Inspector of Missions. Two men assailed me in the dark and I providentially escaped their hands. I ran for safety into a store, where this man and another minister of the same denomination were, and together they saw me safely to the tavern. In the morning the Inspector of missions and myself were going to the Manitoulin Island. He advised me to have the men looked after lest others getting into their hands should fare worse than myself.

Having supplied extensively out of my stock, I returned to Algoma Mills, and finding the prospects for the coming winter not encouraging, we took boat for Sault St. Marie. We found it difficult to obtain a house. We were kindly received by the various congregations.

Having housed my family I attempted to pass through to Detroit and Windsor for the purpose of finding means to continue the work I received a grant of Bibles from the Bible Society at the Sault, and with the remains of former stock I passed the Michigan shore, visited the lumber camps, and passing through the country I came to St. Ignace. Some incidents occurred on the way. At one of the camps my Bibles were taken from me.

After holding religious services those that were not paid for were returned to me. On returning on Monday from another camp I got astray in the woods, but the men found me and put me right. The foreman drawing me to him said, We have a pretty rough crowd here, you are trying to do good to us, and we have need of it. We go from the camp to the drive, and from the drive to the drink, and from the drink to the dogs. We forget home, and home forgets us, and no one cares for us. You are trying to do good to us, and we ought to try to help you. Stay at the camp until we come in to dinner. However little resulted from the proposition.

I started on a journey, they told me it was ten miles. It soon got stormy and snowed heavily. I met the stage and enquired my destination, and they told me I would not reach there that night, it being sixteen miles instead of ten, and was recommended to find a stopping place at one of the houses near. I sought them but found an ungracious reception and I prepared to walk. I soon got bewildered in the darkness, and in among various roads and I concluded I should be lost.

I prayed the Lord earnestly for help. Soon I heard the sound of sleigh bells and I concluded that the Lord had sent some one to my help. I asked the driver if he was going far. I learned he was going to the same place which I wished to get to. I asked him if I could ride with him. He said, I have to travel seventy miles to-night, and if th e sleigh breaks down or the horse gives out I don't know what I will do. I asked him to allow me to run behind and throw my bags in, which he consented to. It was a run of near six miles in the dark over hump and hollow. At last I said I could go no farther. He said, Just hold on for a few minutes and we will be in the yard. I sat down in the snow unable to get into the house. As I attempted to rise I heard him say, You must see to that man or he will freeze out there. I was never more exhausted. Supper was soon ready, and my tea slipped away so fast that the girl was astonished. I was thoroughly parched with the run.

As I went on the road next day I heard people reporting that this man had saved my life. Arriving at St. Ignace winter had fully set in. I could make no sales nor find encouragement, or any way that seemed safe for me to travel. I came down to my last thirty-five cents. I had sent some money home, thinking I could make my way along, but now there was two feet of snow, and a high wind and seventy miles to reach home. The stage fare was five dollars. I concluded the best thing to do was to beat a retreat. I went to the stageman and told him my errand and told him I would like to go to the Soo, but I could not pay him until I got to the other end, and that I would leave him my overcoat as a security for his payment. He said he would see me back. After this a second stageman turned up who unsolicited, offered to take me back free of charge because I was the man from the Canadian side who had been preaching in the camps. I thanked him for his kind offer and told him I had purposed to go by the other stage and my things were there so that I would give him an answer shortly; so I told the first stageman that I had an opportunity to return at a cheaper rate and I thought under the circumstances I ought to avail myself of it. That was all right, he said, but if the other stageman would take me back for three dollars he would do the same. Finally I told him that I could go back free of cost, to which he said if there was any consideration about the matter he thought he was entitled to it, for he had met me according to my own proposition. I admitted that the statement was right, but I was in a strait what to do, as the man had been so kind. So, said he, I'll tell you what to do, go and tell him that you can go back with him on conditions that he pays for your dinner but if not you must go with us, so I was obliged to deliver the message; but the second stageman said he did not mind the ride, but did not wish to pay for the dinner. So I thanked him and told him I was obliged to take the other stage. I gave the stageman No 2 a revised testament as a little acknowledgement of his kind service, and I arrived safely at the Soo, but with an empty pocket, and the registered letter arrived some weeks later, having had to go a long way round, and then by dog teams to the Soo.

1886. On New Year's day I held prayer service in the Dawson Hall, in which public meetings were generally held. A few gathered to give thanks for mercies past and to supplicate His care for days to come. After this I commenced revival services each evening and rented a place for that purpose. This served to set the others going in the same exercise, and Methodist, Presbyterian, and English church joined together. I kept the place open, which I had rented for three months, with little or no encouragement from without, but, like David, I encouraged myself in the Lord, and as early as possible in the spring I held open air services at 9 o'clock Sunday morning. My voice being strong and there being a strong echo a crowd soon gathered, and among them came the constable, somewhat heated, making profane remarks concerning the great noise, taking license because of his office. I said to him, This is the Sabbath morning and if you use profane words on the public highway I will send you to the lock-up. This caused him to be a little laughed at, and I continued my address, but I have an unfeigned horror of all kinds of profanity, and have had many hot contentions in reproving it.

These services were continued till navigation opened when I left by the first boat for Toronto, my son (now deceased) furnishing me with means and obtaining reduced fare by steamboat. The ice had not cleared away and on Manitoulin Island we got aground which caused some delay.

On my arrival at Toronto, I providentially obtained a certificate of integrity signed by twelve of the friends who had kindly helped me in the past, and some had known me for years, most of them well known. This I had published in the Globe. A copy of it is as follows: In the Divine oracle it is written, In the mouth of two or three witnesses every word shall be established, so I felt myself the better prepared to battle for the right. New conflict now showed itself. I had apparently social kindly conversation at the dining table in the tavern with one of the preachers from the Sault with no indication of any trouble but on going to the office of one who had signed the certificate for me, I was shown a statement just published in a religious periodical, stating that my endeavors should not be countenanced, and signed by the person spoken to at the dinner table. My friend told me it was put upon his desk for him to see, which as soon as he saw he threw it away. I learned from Montreal from some who wrote to the writer concerning it, that it was a display of jealousy. In requesting the publisher of the paper to correct the statement he directed me to his lawyer. I asked the advice of a solicitor and after considering it he said, They have attempted the mischief but shielded themselves, but there is nothing legally to take hold of. This is a sample of the brotherly love of some vain talkers which I have had to experience; but it was nothing new, I have at various times had to contend with the same during the 25 years that had passed. Paul and David complained of false brethren and it was an old habit with some even in their days.

I sought some of my friends to review my accounts, but they had not time, so I went to an accountant. I threw off what was coming to me on the first year's work and making no charge for the work of the second beyond what I had received for the books I had sold, I soon paid up the $80.00 balance due from the former year for the scriptures and books I had bought.

REPORT.

From May 10, 1885, to May 10, 1886.

CONTRIBUTIONS BY CASH, BOOKS AND DISCOUNT.

For railway and boat fares	$35 75
Carriage of books,&c	9 70
Printing	11 00
Religious services	6 60
Sundries	10 00
	$73 05
Montreal, Que	$80 38
Lakes Shore Ontario(with item from Toronto)	30 92
Barrie	18 70
Collingwood	16 70
	$146 70

This leaves $73.65 cash, for the support of the Missionary and his family, there have been acts of personal kindness which are not enumerated in the Cash account, for which I express equal thanks. The following is taken from an advertisement in Toronto Evening Globe.

Algoma and North-west Evangelical and Scriptural Colportage Mission.

GEO. BUSKIN, *Missionary.*   TORONTO, May 12th, 1886.
362 Yonge St., Toronto, and Sault St. Marie, Ont.

To confirm the statement previously made in city papers, and that its debt of $85.95 may be removed, and a new supply of Scriptures, &c. furnished, a few friends kindly annex their names.

We, the undersigned residents of the city, being helpers to the Mission from its commencement, and some of us having a previous as well as present knowledge of the Missionary and his work, at his request, and for the encouragement of others to help the work, unite our testimony of confidence in his integrity and work.

(Signed)
F. S. ROBINSON.　　WILLIAM DAVIES.
HENRY PIM.　　　　WM. DAVIES, Jr.
THOS. WOODHOUSE. JOHN FIRSTBROOK.
H. B. GORDON.　　 B. J. HILL.
L. DUNCAN.　　　　A. W. MASON.
May, 11th, 1886.　AIKENHEAD & CROMBIE.

The Toronto *Mail*, of December 6th, 1884, stated from my letter, concerning the summer's work:—"Up to November 3, about 400 Bibles and Testaments have been supplied in eleven languages. Also 500 religious books and over 700 hymn books, with many thousands of religious tracts and magazines, and also sixty religious services held.
From May to Dec. 1st.. 1885.

Extract from Toronto "Mail" May 11th, 1886:

ALGOMA COLPORTAGE MISSION.

"During the past year 164 copies of Scriptures, in seven languages, besides portions; 100 religious books and hymn books, and thousands of religious tracts and magazines have been distributed. Services have been held at many places in the district. The contributions to the Mission during the year have amounted to $158.23.

The Scriptures, &c. have been supplied in the district as follows:—Neighborhood of Algoma Mills, Lake Huron, 89; St. Joseph's and Manitoulin Islands, 49: Neighborhood of Heron Bay, Peninsula Harbor, Jackfish Bay, and West Lake Superior, 49; Neighborhood Sault St. Marie, 44; American Shore, 23; balance on steamboats.

Much larger work might have been done had there been the means at hand to do it—Scriptures might have been supplied in 17 languages— but only a few copies could be obtained in Russian, Finnish, Norwegian and Ojibway Indian, and in most languages except English the supply was not equal to the requirements and tastes of the people. This year I have lacked in English as well as other languages much for which have been requested.

The following are examples of missionary work as taken from his book.

.. June 8, 1885, Serpent River Saw Mills, Lake Huron, Religious Magazines 5cts., Life of Spurgeon, 20cts., Precept upon

Precept, 50cts., Religious papers, 5cts., Health lectures, 30c, Testament and Psalms 90cts., Bible 35cts., 2 Hymn books with music 15cts each, 1 French testament given, 2 Bible Class primers 15cts. each, Bible 75cts., Bible 90cts., Bible 65cts., Hymn book with music 20cts., 2 French Bibles 35cts. each, Testament and Psalms 75cts., tracts and magazines distributed, Religious Service held, this being the 5th visit in 2 years, each having similar evidences, the foregoing being two days' work including rowing boat 16 miles.

Jackfish Bay, Lake Superior, July 19, 1885. C. P. R. French Bible 35cts., French Testament, 15cts., Testament 10 cts., 3 religious services in the open air, Gaelic Testament 15 cts.; Bunyan's Grace Abounding, Gaelic, 60cts.; Dr. Guthrie Christian's great interest, Gaelic 75cts.; Peninsula Harbor, German Bible, 35cts.; Bible, 25cts.; Hymn book, 10cts., Italian Testament, 10cts., Italian Testament, 20cts. cost 40cts.; Hymn book, 10cts., Bible, 10cts. cost 30cts., Bible given 15cts., 2 Testaments 10cts. each, Bible, 15cts., Bible, 25cts., Bible, 15cts given, Bible, 15cts., Swedish Testament, 25cts. cost 30cts., Testament 5cts. given, 2 Bibles, 25cts. each, given, Bible, 25cts. Received $1.75 contribution, no Protestant religious service held for 12 months.

Cascade Silver Lead Mine, Nov. 24th, 1885, Lake Huron, 21 Scriptures and books sold in 4 languages and three portions, and a variety of religious literature supplied, religious service held, contribution $6.58, no minister of any kind there for 2 years.

No higher price has been asked for bibles and books, than marked by the Bible Society, Tract Society, and Standard Publishing Co., sometimes they have been sold for less, and sometimes given, to facilitate the extension of Christian knowledge.

Thanking the many kind friends for their aid by word and deed, and for contributions of religious literature and shall be glad to be further remembered in this way.

In this, my 4 years endeavour to obtain the means to sustain this agency of Christian knowledge and grace, I do so in the name and dependence upon our common Lord who has said, "All power is given unto me in Heaven and in Earth," respectfully asking the prayers and co-operation of all who fear Him. The evidences of this year have been as in the past years, men are engaged by scores and hundreds on public works and private enterprise for months and years together, and their soul's welfare is not considered so as to seek to reach them in this matter. An official on the C. P. R. R. said to me: "I am convinced upon evidence that the only way to overcome the Sabbath labour is to maintain the Sunday religious services." There need be no wonder if men stray far from grace when the means of grace is not extended to them. Let us then seek to have our feet shod with the preparation of the gospel of peace, and above all put on Charity, which is the bond of perfectness.

Since September 1882, 2000 Scriptures, Religious books and Hymn books have been supplied in this district, similar to the example given in this statement, besides nearly 10,000 religious tracts, magazines and papers, and more than 200 religious services have been held.

Hoping that the above statement may receive your consideration and enlist your cordial support,
    I am,
        Yours in the Gospel,
            GEO. BUSKIN,
        SAULT STE. MARIE, ALGOMA, ONT.

I had resolved if possible to go to England and seek some organization who would in whole or part take up the work; so when at Montreal a friend obtained the opportunity for me to work my way over, receiving 2 sovereigns and a return ticket. I arrived at my own town of Bristol, but sought there to no purpose, save receiving 30 or 40 shillings, but found it as before, that unless you can be in the slide of the denominational groove whether you stand or fall there are few that care, be you new or old connection, or antiquated, or of latest novelty, unless you have the denominational shibboleth twang, and cut and ride in the denominational Sedan chair if you cannot swim you can sink, the denominational life-boat is for the select few; and few they are that would bemoan you; in fact Elijah-like, you are considered "he that troubleth Israel," and I think if the Lord Himself should visit the churches to-day as in the days that are past they would see no beauty that they would desire Him. I am persuaded that the whole church fabric, as it exists to-day must be pulled down to the ground, because there is not in it the Holy Ghost subjection, nor yet the proper measure of the fruits brought forth by the profession. It is largely dwarfed, blighted, and perverted. The Spirit is rejected and Jude's words must be fulfilled: "Woe unto them: they have gone in the way of Cain and ran greedily after the error of Balaam for re-

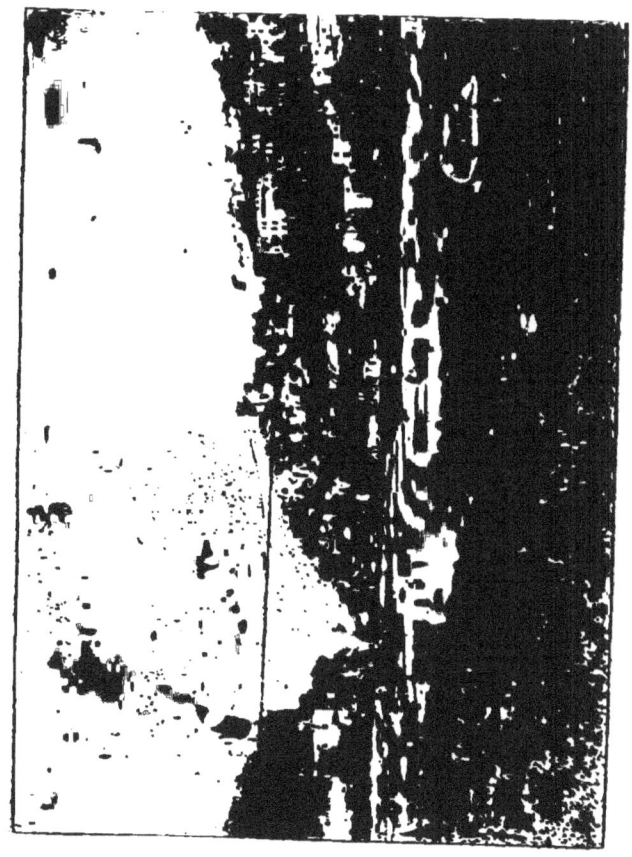

River Avon. Hotwells and Clifton, where many of my earlier days were spent.

ward and perished in the gainsaying of Core." These may seem hard words, but when the tree had nothing but leaves the Master cursed it, and to the Scribes and Pharisees Christ said, "Woe unto you," and that woe fully came not many years later when Jerusalem was overthrown. Will the Scribes and Pharisees of to-day fare better who have the Lord's name near in their mouths but He is far from their hearts? The prophecy of Enoch must yet be fulfilled, "Behold the Lord cometh with ten thousands of his saints to execute judgement upon all." What then will be the end of the shepherds who feed themselves but not the flock. The ministry of the gospel has largely degenerated from the Holy Ghost's qualifications found in Romans, chapters 8 and 12, 1 Corinthians 12,13,14, Ephesians 3,4,5, 1 Thessalonians 2, 1 Timothy 3,4,5, also 2 Timothy, the Epistle of Titus, 1 Peter 5:1-5, 2 Peter 2, 3 John, Rev. 1-4, also chapters 17, 18, and 22. Christ the great Shepherd of the sheep, when pursuing his ministry, went through the land of Israel. He sent also into every city into which also He Himself should come, the Apostles, and many of the disciples went everywhere preaching the Word. The priests in Israel had their fields as well as their houses and many of them did their plowing, sowing and reaping, so that they had bread enough and to give to him that needeth, and Paul did the same in his way as an example, and our Lord was a carpenter until He became an evangelist, and we may rightly conclude that, while pursuing his carpentering He, on the Sabbath and at other times, attended the synagogue and read and expounded the Scriptures.

But the day is very far spent and the night at hand. It is now too late to do much reproving to profit, but if men would spend less time in their literary flower gardens, and get out into the open fields of honest toil and service, they would do much better. Some men fish with an angle, but they cannot do much more than serve their own tables. The Apostles were not artistic characters at fishing, they used nets, worked hard, and supplied themselves and the markets, too, for people's needs. It is not too late for the professed gospel fishermen to put away their fancy hooks and flies, and get into the gospel ship and let down the nets for a draught. There will be less of sport but more of service, wealth eternal, and renown. I do pity and despise many of the poor helpless professors of the gospel to whom I have been concerning Christ's cause.

I was obliged to tell one in honesty that to my judgment

he was more capable of making infidels than converts to Christ. Though there be the gift of prophesy and understanding all mystery and all knowledge, and having all faith so as to remove mountains, but lacking the grace of our Lord Jesus Christ (which the so-called fathers of the church have mystified and crippled by calling it by the senseless name of charity). These gifts profit the possessor no more than they did David's counsellor, Ahithophel, who though his counsel was as the oracle of God, came to a fool's end, his conscience being to him an unconquerable adversary. 2 Samuel 16th and 17th chapters.

I hereby insert my previously printed account of going to England, and the heartless reception I met with from institutions and men, in the face of the great blazing renown there maintained of wealth, character and profession, both individual and associate. The following is the

STATEMENT OF RESULTS

of an application made in England to obtain help for the Algoma and North West Evangelical and Scriptural Colportage Mission, and also to obtain a stock of Scriptures, Religious Books, Hymn Books and Tracts, besides other grants: In the hope that by God's blessing it may serve to stimulate the interest in Canada of the Algoma and North West Gospel and Colportage Mission, I briefly and respectfully acquaint the helpers of the same of my application in England to the various organizations for the sustaining of Christian missions, and the extension of Christian knowledge, to obtain their aid, that a greater work might be done. The many ties that bind the old and this new land seemed to indicate that there would be a glad response. There are family, friendly and national ties, traffic and wealth, a great profession of earnest attachment to the Lord Jesus and His word, that should make our interest one. There are also the pre-eminent resources of Biblical literature which are theirs. There is with them the stores of ages of knowledge and wealth. These were the reasons for judging that whether with success or failure, the effort was worth making, to obtain some of the superabundances in some quarters, to apply to the necessities of the other, and also to awaken if possible a greater interest on behalf of those who are poor and needy, especially the spiritually neglected.

In those far off and out of the way places, it is important that by the supply of the nutriment of the Word of God, and such literature as shall build up Christian character, the good seeds of grace and truth sown in early days among many, might not be caught away by the adversary of souls, but might take root and bear fruit unto life eternal. There being twenty languages spoken through the country, makes it a matter requiring direct application, and careful consideration.

Last summer a Christian Icelander, a poor hard-working man, to whom I sold an Iceland Bible, said, "I have been five years in the country, and did not know where to obtain an Iceland Bible." Those who have been taught to read Gaelic have said, "The Scriptures in Gaelic have more force to me than in English." Another to whom I sold a large Bible said, "I have been waiting years for this, and now money will not buy it." Because of failing to obtain in Canada Scriptures in many languages for many hundreds of men, I wrote nearly two years since to eminent men and associations in London, England, to obtain that which was necessary, but failed. If the work were but in the interest of the Indians only, it would be well worth the support asked for it.

By way of illustrating the condition of some of the Indians, I would state, that ten years since, while calling (to do some good among the Indians,) at Parry Island, Georgian Bay (an Indian reserve), a native teacher on the Island said to me, "The Indians in the villages are all heathen; you can do nothing with them, they don't understand anything." There has been done among them, since then, however, a good work of instruction and improvement. Two years since, a missionary at Nepigeon, Lake Superior, said to me, "the Indians a hundred miles back from here are heathen and are hostile to Christians." I have also found that they are numerous in the districts I have visited, and in many cases are ignorant, idle, uncultivated and uncared for, and the only thing really to suit their condition, is the grace and truth of the Lord Jesus Christ. But before they can properly value the Scriptures, they must be taught to read, and those who can read, require the same helps that are found so necessary for the white man, and the white child.

My journey to England was provided for by my own labor and resources, without any deductions from contributions previously made. I left Montreal July 6th, and landed 12 days later, in the famous old city of Bristol, whose business relations with Canada are large, and where religious professions and operations have been, and still are of great renown.

From all the organizations to which I made application, (6 in number,) as yet I have received no contributions in the way of literature. I called two public meetings, posting more than 200 large bills, and in the Bristol Times and Mirror inserted the following advertisement: "Monday, July 26th.—All interested in christian work are kindly invited to attend missionary meetings at Pavey's rooms, 35 Victoria street, Clifton, to-day, Monday, afternoon at 3.30, evening at 7.30, for the furtherance of a gospel and and colportage mission in the Algoma and North-West districts of Canada." After 10 days' of hard work calling on leading clergy and business men, I left for London, having received in cash £1 14s or about $9.00, and 12 gospel portions in French, and a few small books. A suggestion worth remembering was made by a dissenting deacon, "that it would be as reasonable for Canadians to help reclaim the people in the back slums of England, as that they should help a work of evangelization in the backwoods of Canada." But his wisdom, if that is the right name, ended with words. I hope we may be able, by God's blessing, to begin where he left off, and find the answer to the important question, Who is my neighbor? and bring that answer into practice.

Upon starting for London, friends from Montreal sent me the following letters:—

I have just time to enclose you a note to the Secretary of London Y. M. C. A., Exeter Hall, which I trust may be of service to you in your arduous labors. May the Lord who has led you so far, carry you through, and open many hearts to assist you. Yours in the love of Jesus,

N. MACINTOSH.

Y. M. C. A., VICTORIA SQUARE, MONTREAL, JULY 14, '86
Mr. Edmund J. Kennedy, Secretary,
    Exeter Hall, London, England.

Permit me to introduce the bearer, Mr. Buskin, who visits your city at this time. He is engaged in christian work in the back districts of Canada, and would be glad to have the privilege of attendance at your rooms and meetings.

Yours faithfully,
D. A. BUDGE, Secretary.

This favor I found helpful and prepared the way for the following statement:

AN APPEAL.

To the Nobility and Christian Public of the People of London and vicinity.

Your kind aid is respectfully solicited on behalf of a Colportage and Gospel Mission, Algoma and the North-west District of Canada, by the missionary, Geo. Buskin.

A brief statement of its operations are given in the accompanying circular. Any communication can be addressed to him, care of Mr. Burn, Y. M. C. A., 186 Aldersgate street, London, or Mrs. E. E. Pavey, 35 Victoria street, Clifton, Bristol.

Which I used with about 500 circulars describing the work done during the past 4 years. I wrote 12 statements to organizations similar to the following, which was sent to Secretary of Religious Tract Society.

Care MR. BURN, Sec. Y. M. C. A.,
186 Aldersgate st., London, E. C. Aug. 4th.
GENTLEMEN:

I shall be thankful if your Committee will kindly make a grant of books and tracts to aid in the prosecution and extension of the Mission work stated upon the enclosed circular. To obtain help for the furtherance of the same, the way has been opened for me to come to this country. I am not alone in the desire that help should be sought here, but others who have their part in it, have concluded that to make a personal appeal in England is the best thing to be done. There are in the district 20 languages spoken. The examples given in the circulars are the general aspect of laborers and back settlers through the district. The people are poor, as all new settlers are, especially when they have 5 or 6 months' winter to contend with. Gentlemen, yours truly in the Gospel,
——— GEO. BUSKIN.

THE RELIGIOUS TRACT SOCIETY, 56 PATERNOSTER ROW,
London, Aug. 12th, 1886.
George Buskin, in care Mrs. E. Pavey,
35 Victoria st., Clifton, Bristol.

The Committee have much pleasure in voting you a supply of tracts in various languages, (12) for your interesting and important work in Canada. For languages not included in our grant it would be well for you to apply to the Toronto Tract Society. With best wishes, I am faithfully yours,
- SAMUEL GREEN.

BRITISH AND FOREIGN BIBLE SOCIETY, 146 Queen Victoria st,,
London, E. C. Aug. 19th, 1886.
Mr. George Buskin, Dear Sir,

The Committee have responded to your application for a

grant in aid of the Gospel Mission, which you are carrying on among Canadian Pacific Railway men, &c., by a grant of 300 Gospel portions, subject to the approval of our Auxiliary in Toronto, the Upper Canada Bible Society. If you will kindly call upon Mr. J. Harvie, the Secretary, on your return to Toronto, he will arrange with you as to the grant.
I am, dear Sir, yours truly,
CHARLES FINCH.

(The grant referred to above has been received.—Consisting of 125 portions in 6 languages, 50 Testaments in 12 languages, and 2 Bibles, making about 14 languages. G. B.)

From MRS. C. H. SPURGEON, WESTWOOD, Upper Norwood.
Aug. 9th, 1886.
Dear Sir:
You are not eligible for a grant from my book fund in the usual way, but I shall be very pleased to give you 250. of Mr. Spurgeon's sermons, if they can be distributed among those you labor for. If you take the enclosed note to Messrs Passmore and Alabaston, 4 Paternoster Buildings, Paternoster Row, E. C., they will supply you with the number stated. Wishing you every success in your good work.
Believe me, truly yours,
(Mrs. C. H.) SUSIE SPURGEON.

The Sunday School Union kindly contributed £1.00 worth of small books and papers, more especially adapted for children.

Having during three weeks made many personal and written applications to representative men of Christian work, with the same diligence that I have pursued it in Canada, also taking offices and wholesale houses, I found myself destitute of money to provide food, or to pay my lodging, much less further the Gospel in the wilds of the beloved Colony of Canada.

In the kind providence of the Lord, a good friend from Montreal furnished me the means of immediate return.

This will answer any who think or say I abuse the confidence placed in me. As the good Master has opened a broad land before us, full of his goodness, let us seek grace to serve him in it, that his blessing, which is life for evermore, may be with us through the knowledge of Jesus Christ. Though the expectations of the journey have not at this time been realized, it cannot fail to profit while the promise holds good,

"Your labor is not in vain in the Lord." Respectfully asking the continued aid of your prayers and support.
Yours in the service of the Lord Jesus Christ,
GEO. BUSKIN.

However, marked providences were manifested on my behalf. After a stay there of about three weeks, I again returned and landed at Montreal early in September, visited Ottawa and went straight to Sault Ste. Marie, and for a time did extensive and profitable work, many persons having come to the Sault by reason of the settled purpose of the C. P. R. to build the Sault branch. At one lumber mill I sold 35 copies of Scriptures and portions and 89 books, receiving $21.75 for them, and conducting religious services. At another I supplied 34 Scriptures and 50 books, receiving $18.46 for them. Also held two religious services. This was the work of two days in each place. These were house to house sales. I will let those who read estimate the labor and the possible results of it.

AN EXTRACT FROM THE ALGOMA PIONEER, Oct. 8th, 1886. "Mr. Buskin the street preacher took his stand on Sunday morning and afternoon and preached a sound scriptural salvation doctrine. Good results must inevitably follow all faithful labor, no matter how uninviting the field, and this gospel preacher will be no exception to the rule in the day when every man's work shall be tried what sort it is."

The supplies of Biblical literature was much larger than the former year, being 350 Scriptures and portions in five languages, and 500 books, besides distribution of tracts, and conducting religious services. The contributions in cash and books were $746.31, of which $76.84 was from England. There was paid out of the contributions, $308.80 for printing, travelling, back debts and sundries, leaving $437.51 for the support of the missionary and family. Through an oversight, but not wilfully, the moneys received for sales of books, were not entered in this or former accounts, though not mentioned, there was no design to abuse the confidence of any, whether supporters or opposers of the work. This is evident from the amounts of money that remained for the missionary each year after paying expenses. This year's account was reviewed by Mr. Josiah Burnett, accountant, 50 Adelaide st., Toronto, in whose hands it was placed by reason of the inability of friends to spare time, to investigate them, as had been done previously for two years.

1887. This brings us to the fourth year of the work, 1887.

Among other matters a mission room was built at the Sault, 13 by 25 feet, as a depository for the books and a meeting room for the strangers at the Sault. Work being very active in the construction of the Algoma branch of the C. P. R., for a time I employed a man to visit the lumber camps, but found him unsuitable for the work. The travelling during the year was west of the Sault to French River and Georgian Bay, in a circle of about 700 miles, visiting many camps, mills and homes. The following is a sample of sales at one of the railway camps: 14 Bibles in five languages, and 12 books, also conducting religious services.

The sales of this year numbered: Of scriptures, 900 in whole or part, and of books 1,300, making together 2,200 copies in ten languages. We may say, with such seed sowing, what will the harvest be? The donations of this year were $640.05, out of which were paid to other persons, as travelling, helper, building, &c., $351.49, which left $288.56 for the missionary. The money received for books sold was $300.00. The accounts for this year were certified by J. Rowland, accountant, 12 Wellington st., west, Toronto.

Of these donations $90.00 came largely from the men on the construction of the Algoma branch. Being at Algoma Mills at Christmas, I conducted morning religious service at the schoolhouse. I was surprised on returning to the boarding house that they had a gift for me of about $14.00, beside other sums which came to me before and after. It is more pleasing to receive unsolicited aid in Christ's work than to constrain it.

1888. Now we come to the fifth year. This year's printed reports being lost, the best that I can do is to say that the donations together were $932.17, as taken from the collecting book; and by referring to other reports, I find that the number of scriptures and books supplied during this year amounted to 1670. I find that up to September, 871 books were sold, for which was paid $154.39. The fire which burned the premises in 1896 is probably the cause of having no report left for that year.

1889. Passing on to the sixth year, there had been published 7 various editions of Scripture books for use in the work. French, German, Italian, and English, which have been found helpful as educators and profitable as Christian instructors, One contributor told me that one in English had been the means of a little girl's conversion, and that he wished to encourage me in the work and gave me his second five dollar donation. Of another edition I found a copy in the hands of two persons in the City of Quebec on my first visit there, years after their publication, and though sold at 10c. per copy, one told me he would not be without it for fifty cents. Some of the Italian books have been sent to Italy and have been used here in many Italian homes, some schools, and in districts far away. The same results are shown in the French and German languages.

The number of scriptures supplied this year were about 285 and 676 Scriptural books in six languages, besides distribution of religious tracts, and conducting religious services. The donations for the year $952.87 being the largest amount yet received. The amount expended was $1,320.00, there being on hand, books purchased and mission printed books, mission room, mission ground, horse, etc,—Value $805.00. Since 1882 there had been supplied by the Mission agency, 7,631 scriptures and books in 17 languages. JOHN MACKINTOSH,
Accountant.

1890. A sample of the work at Garden River Lumber camp, Jan. 6th and 7th, 1890: Two Bibles, 11 Testaments and 25 books.

On leaving one camp to go to the other, I got into a heavy snow storm. I started to walk long before daylight, expecting to meet teams on the way going to the camp, but that day they took another course. The way was long and the books grew heavier all the time, so it appeared to me, and the snow got deeper and softer and finally I had to hang one of my bags to a tree, for I could carry it no farther. No other man did I meet travelling the road I went, save at the cross road, miles behind. Some time later I had to hang up another bag and tug myself along and had the road been much longer, I should have been fast in the snow myself. However, by God's help, I reached the camp sometime in the afternoon, and after getting warmed and some food and a rest, I returned to find my bags of books, which was not easy work by reason of so much snow having fallen.

I conducted religious services in the first camp, and I suppose I also did at the second. In all these places there is a mixture of good and evil. One man there bought nine 3ct. Testaments;another showed his mind by causing me to hear his words at midnight, among which he said of myself; "The old Jesuit ! What does he want in here ? I'll see he and his bags over the dump in the morning," which meant a drop over the rocks about sixty feet; but the midnight tale and the morning one did not agree, for another I suppose heard his words, and the man who bought the nine testaments said to me after breakfast, "Come, friend, I'll help you with the bags and see you safe from this camp before I go to work." On the way he said, "This is the worst camp I have ever been in." Their profanity was such that he told them he would take a 20 mile tramp and get a summons out for them unless it was stopped. However, I have been in and out of many camps without suffering greatly. The Lord be praised for His care.

I delivered among them the word of God through exhortation, as well as the voice of praise and supplication and Bibles and books. I have been sorely strained at times on these journeys to keep on my legs—from one of them I made 40 miles in one day, 30 miles I walked and 10 miles I rode, with stinging frost and deep snow, to renew my supplies. On another occasion I went on snow shoes and lost my way and had to return on my track; and falling in the snow was too much exhausted to rise, until some one came to my help. In the Garden River district I have had many novel experiences. Once walking there, a journey of 12 miles with heavy load, in deep snow, to reach some camps, without money to pay for food, about 5 o'clock I gave out and had to ask at a house to stay for the night. I was welcome to food, but there was no bed to be had. After supper and a rest, I took up my load again and tramped to the camp, six miles farther. I was well pleased with the night's results, in supplying the Word of Life.

Near the same place, in summer time, I was picked up with my load, by a man driving with a buckboard. I had wriggled along till I could get no farther. He brought me to the steamboat dock. To the warehouseman he said, "I picked up this man and his bags, lying on the roadside." "No wonder", said the dockman, "he puts more on his back, than I would put on my horse."

On another occasion in the same neighborhood, I was weary with my load and vexed by reason of labor without success, but at the last call, I sold a $1.00 large print Bible for a present by a young woman to her parents, Bunyan's Pilgrim's Progress and Holy War, Uncle Tom's Cabin, a $9.00 family Bible, and what more I do not now remember, but I left the house with about $14.00 more than when I entered and relieved of some of my load. Such experiences as these have been not infrequent.

Once I went on horseback because I was so faint. I had continually to pray the Lord to give me strength to reach the journey's end, which He in mercy did. Now I think I will leave the reports to tell the rest of the toils, until I can write them better, if the Providence of God permits. But to those who accuse our conversation in Christ as deceit, I would ask, how much more have you toiled and sacrificed and suffered? If you boast of strength of character, how much more diligent and devoted have you been, and if wise, has it been in meekness of wisdom, or like the Corinthians, puffed up because of the gifts. But charity edifieth. That is not almsgiving, but charity does not dispense with gifts, nor almsgiving, but sanctifies both. Charity is as the sun, the reflection of the Divine, around which as satellites, the gifts may sparkle, but it is charity that must shine with rays of purity, peace and compassion, easy to be entreated, without partiality and hypocrisy.

We would say to one and all who read, if thou canst not do better, at least go and do thou likewise. There was a difference between Israel and the mixed multitude who went up out of Egypt with them, as there is between the soldier and the camp follower, or the stage-playing, liveried soldier and the warrior of the field. If, by any means and the blessing of the Lord, this record may serve to make some strong in faith, and quit themselves like men, in the Lord's battle against the hosts of darkness, the praise and honor be to the Lord, for by grace we are saved through faith, and that not of ourselves; it is the gift of God, not of works, least any man should boast, for we are His workmanship, created anew in Christ Jesus unto good works which God hath before ordained that we should walk in them. And again with Paul we all should say, "yet not I, but the grace of God, which was with me." Old Saul was dead and buried, new man Paul occupied His house, and so it must be with us. "I can do all things through Christ which strengtheneth me." There are many who boast themselves of other persons' labors, instead of being humbled under the sense of obligation to God and their fellows, for what has a man that he has not received. Before honor is humility, and if people will not take upon them the suffering of reproach and the labor of the cross of Christ, what claim can they make to the throne of His glory. If they refuse subjection now to Him, when will they be anything else but rebels to His authority.

I must for the present, respectfully request that the reports shall make up the balance of the apology for the work of the mission to those persons who by reason of their haughtiness of spirit, object to their privileged assumptions and positions being encroached upon. An endeavor at politeness occasions the expression of apology, which, after all, in this connection is but an accommodating expression to those with whom grace is lacking. Seeing we must all appear before the judgment seat of Christ that our works may be tried of what sort it is, let us continually seek grace, not only to say, "Lord, Lord," but to do the things He commands, which is the evidence that He dwells in us and we in Him. The firstfruits of His Spirit is love unfeigned, not in word only, but in deed and truth. "He that loveth Him that begat, loveth him also that is begotten." The grapes do not bear thorns, nor the fig tree thistles, but there is a lot of thorny, thistly profession, which only seems to choke out the life of those who attempt to swallow it.

, G. BUSKIN,
Colportage Mission,
202 King st. E., Toronto, Ont.
17 Eagle st. Rochester, N. Y.

Reports of the Work Done Since '89.

Our last report given was that of 1889, which was the sixth year. We here give a brief report of each year's work up to the end of last year.

SEVENTH YEAR'S REPORT.

1890. The number of Scriptures supplied have been about 263 in 8 languages, and 714 Scriptural books. Religious tracts and magazines which have been bought and donated have been freely supplied, more than 50 religious services have been held in camps, open air, etc; the total number of scriptures and scriptural books supplied since September, 1882, being 8,608, in seventeen languages, and 512 religious services held, also nine small scriptural books published in five languages. The contributions for the year have been $976.86, the amoun expended $1,338.30; the liabilities are $1,029.71, the assets $1,160.00, including mission house and lots, mission furniture and supplies, horse, waggon, sleigh, etc., the amount contribu ted for the work since March 10th, 1884, being $5,453.05.

JOHN MACKINTOSH, Accountant.

From a letter received, Feb. 3, 1891, from three men, late attendants at the canal mission room, who left the Soo to seek work, we learn that our work among laboring men is helpful: "We stayed at Garden River at an Indian boarding house. We had supper and a meal in the morning of salt pork, bread and tea, and when George went and asked him how much it would be he said he would only charge us fifty cents each; he said he charged us nothing for the bed. I wish you had been there; the beds and the cold, it was not fit for a dog to sleep there, and the next night we had not enough to buy a meal. We got to Bruce about six o'clock, so we went to a hotel and told the landlord we were strapped. Well, he said he would see what he could do, but he let us stay all night; and in the morning we were about dead with hunger, when a young man told us to go and get our breakfast and he would pay for it, so we got it and felt good after and went out on the Government road and struck this job, (paper wood cutting). Tell Reub that we are all well at present. Give our love to him and Mr. Buskin. Tell them that we have prayer-meetings once or twice a week." I leave these letters to plead for themselves. It shows that the hearts of some are reached by the grace of God, and that some in pocket, as well as in spirit, are among the poor and needy in the Christian wilderness and in the wilderness of Algoma.

During the past year I spent much time among the laborers upon the Sault Canal, and last October opened a Mission Room for them close to the work, where prayer and praise have for some time ascended daily to God, and my confidence is that those prayers will in God's time be answered.

While thankful for the great mercies received from our Heavenly Father's hand, I have also to groan beneath the burdens and griefs from which I have been unable to escape.

The spring of 1889 which opened to me with cheering prospects early became overcast, and gathering clouds increased, and have left a settled gloom. While mourning the loss of Toronto friends and helpers, I have now to mourn the loss of my own best friend and helper—my wife, who was taken with a sudden sickness in May and died 17th of January, 1890. By God's grace she could sing a few hours before her death, a song she had often sung in health, but never to me before with import so distinct—

> I need Thee, precious Jesus,
> For I am full of sin;

My soul is dark and guilty;
My heart is dead within.
I need the cleansing fountain,
Where I can always flee;
The blood of Christ most precious.
The sinner's perfect plea.

I also had the burdens of back debts, losses and delays of goods in transit, the slowness also with which purchases have been made and paid for, also contention occasioned by jealous rivalry—lamentable to say that such and Christian profession can go together; but our work is forward, by God's help and blessing, and not to look behind nor stay in all the plain (Gen. xix. 17), and by grace say with the apostle, none of these things move me, knowing in whom I have believed. I am thankful to say that during the year French and English and Indian and English hymns have been published for the work, and other translations are also necessary, and I trust in due time to be able to go forward with them, trusting the Lord and the good will of His servants that all responsibilities will be duly met, and the work carried forward and enlarged, that all the ends of the earth may see the salvation of our God.

I am thankful to say that I found more generous practical help the past year than at any previous time.

The petition prepared last year for the Dominion Parliament, asking their help, especially in the interest of the Indians has been handed to Mr. Wood for presentation, signed by two hundred and forty names. I could have had it signed by many more (even ten times as many), but I found it difficult to do several things at the same time without encroaching too much upon the time of our kind friends, and also my memory often failed me at the proper moment. As yet no answer has been received, so as yet I suppose it has not been presented.

My journeys during the past year have been round the shore of Lake Huron and on the Manitoulin Island. I have been prevented from extending my journeys for lack of means. I will by God's help endeavor to lay up a reserve fund to meet the cost and risk of going farther from home. Having so many payments to make, my pockets are nearly always empty.

Among the first work done during the year was to give a Bible to a young woman who was without one and had no money to buy, and who said that when she was a child her mother used daily to read the Scripture to her children; she afterwards came to the Mission Room service and told me that it was four years since she had been to any religious service before; also another who had absented himself for sixteen years. Some strays are occasionally met in this way to whom we are privileged to speak a word in season.

Many Finlanders have been met with during the year and supplied with Scriptures; one, though under the influence of strong drink, would not lose the opportunity of buying a Testament and Psalms in his own language. The Lord make it a blessing as He has done before in similar circumstances; another Fin, who many months before bought a copy of the New Testament, made me a present of fifty cents which I entered among the contributions. "Cast thy bread upon the waters, and thou shalt find it after many days (give a portion to seven and also to eight) for thou knowest not the way of the Spirit."

EIGHTH YEAR'S REPORT.

1891. The number of Scriptures and portions supplied has been about 378 in eleven languages, and 1,638 scriptural books, for which have been received $440.15. Of these Scriptures and books 1,760 were supplied in the Algoma District and 256 outside. There were about 50 religious services conducted in the districts, besides Scripture reading, prayer and exhortation in many homes and houses, and large quantities of religious tracts given, also Scriptures and books of the value of $25.75. The contributions for the year have been $1,186.90; disbursements, $2,169.11; liabilities, $939.69; assets, $720— including mission lots and buildings, mission furniture and supplies of books, etc. Since September, 1882, 10,368 Scriptures and scriptural books have been supplied in 17 languages, and many hundreds supplied outside; also 562 religious services conducted in the district, and over 10,000 religious tracts distributed. The united contributions for the work since March 24th, 1884, have been $6,739.95.

JOHN MACKINTOSH, Accountant.

During the past year the Scriptures and books have been supplied in 11 languages, viz.: English, French, Gaelic, German, Swedish, Danish, Finnish, Pole, (Ojibway) Indian, Hebrew and Italian. I have not produced any new books during the year, as I have not the means to meet the expense, but some are on the way for publication which are necessary for the work. A four paged tract has been published for distribution, entitled "Tracts for the People." The seeds of truth and kindness need be freely sown, and it will be gratifying to o. r friends to know that the first edition of 2,000 of the Scripture Reader in English has been used, and I purpose improving it and getting out another edition as soon as possible; also the first edition of 1,000 copies of the Gospel of John in tne Douay and King James versions are nearly exhausted. Many of the contributors have been pleased to receive a copy of these publications, as well as many sales have been made. I am constrained to say that there should be a more active interest in the spiritual enlightenment of our French neighbours, by supplying them with helpful Christian literature, cheap, attractive and instructive, which may give to them an evidence of an unfeigned and loving interest in their spiritual, moral and social welfare.

The petition to the Dominion Government on behalf of the Mission work was presented last summer by Mr. Wood, M.P., but I have not as yet heard if it has received consideration, they being too much occupied with other matter last year to do so.

The box of Mission property lost by the Canadian Pacific Railroad Co., Dec. 1, 1890, value $135, has not been returned, and the suit against them for recovery of damages was thrown out, although the jury gave judgment for $108, the Company finding a legal way of escape, representing that the portion of the Algoma branch of the Canadian Pacific road on which it was lost was not theirs, yet they advertise it as such and also issue tickets for the same in their name. It is in vain for me to pursue them further, they have so many hiding places from justice; but let them repent of their deeds lest finally they should have to call upon the rocks and mountains to fall upon them and hide them from the presence of God and the wrath of the Lamb. When righteousness shall be put to the line and judgment to the plummet, they will not laugh then at beating a poor man out of his rights.

NINTH YEAR'S REPORT.

1892. The number of Scriptures and Scripture books supplied in the district during the past summer has been about 1,200, in 7 languages, for which have been received nearly $200 including payment of some back debts, $15 worth has been given, 20 religious services have also been conducted there. Since September, 1882, about 11,500 scriptures and scriptural books have been supplied in the district in 17 languages and entered iu the book of mission sales. Many have been given that have not been entered; 583 religious services have been conducted

Preaching at the Halfway House between Herford and Worcester on a Saturday night.

there over many hundred miles of the country, and many thousands of religious tracts and magazines also have been distributed. Twelve various editions of small scriptural books, necessary for rudimental Christian instruction, have been published in five languages for the work, numbering 15,500 copies, many of which have been largely and widely circulated, and seven other editions in four languages, numbering 7,500 copies, are in course of publication. The united contributions commencing March 24th, 1884, to the present time have been $8,295.50.

     WM. SMALLWOOD, Accountant,
      22 and 24 Lombard St., Toronto, Ont.

I have been hindered from doing more in the district by lack of means to meet the various expenses and debts, and also for want of practical personal help. I own with gratitude and thankfulness the sustaining and tender mercy of our loving Lord and Saviour, at whose word and in whose great name I pursue the work and rejoice in the fellowship of the gospel with all those who have so kindly helped me with their substance and their prayers. I have often been pressed sorely with my little load of cares, and been very weary in the little service I have rendered, yet I can truly say, the Lord has not left me nor forsaken me at any time. The following fact will indicate many of my experiences, which oftentimes are not joyous—but light breaks in on the darkness, and indicates our past labors are not lost. When packing the books to begin this year's work, and not knowing how to find money for the journey and to meet expenses of starting, I received payment, unexpected and unsought, for books supplied years ago, far back on the shores of Lake Superior, which enables me to go forward. The contributions of the year have been larger than any previous one, but the responsibilities have been greater. The following will be gratifying to the friends who have helped:

    93 Elm St., Toronto, Ont., Nov. 15th, 1892.

We, the undersigned Superintendents, Teachers and Scholars of the Italian Mission, thankfully acknowledge the benefit we derive from the use of the Italian and English Reader, published by the Algoma and North-west Evangelical and Colportage Mission and which we could not well do without, and trust that by God's blessing it may be a means of extensively imparting the knowledge of a Saviour's love. Signed: Michele Basso, R. Reynolds, Geo. Rowland, W. D. Stark, John H. Cornyn,.

Geo. J. Gipson, Christine Muldoon, Annie Mellick, Julia Trevaill, Lewis Gates.

TENTH YEAR'S REPORT.

1893. The number of Scriptures and Scriptural books supplied in the district by the mission during the past summer have been 849 in 6 languages, a few others have been sent in German and English. The cash received for those supplied, including a few back payments, has been $152.27. Those given in whole or part has amounted to $12.80. Also 568 have been supplied outside the district, which have been made note of, for which $27.44 has been received and $4.80 worth has been given; also many hundreds of our published books have been given to contributors. The religious services were conducted in the district in various parts, and many also have been held outside the district in various parts, also at the rooms, 202 King St. East, Toronto. Friends have conducted prayer and exhortatory services until disturbed beyond measure by disorderly boys, and the doors obliged to be closed, awaiting better capabilities of preserving order.

The united contributions of the year have been $1419.12, and the amount received by sales $179.81; Disbursements, $2,012.52; and the assets over liabilities, $1,085.00. The number of scriptures, scriptural and helpful books supplied in the district by the mission and missionary since 1892 has been 12,359 in 17 languages, and 609 religious services conducted. Also much work of a similar kind has been done outside the district, and 18 various editions of scriptural and rudimental books of instruction have been published by the mission and for its use in 5 languages, numbering 35,900 copies when all are finished. These have been freely used and found to be helpful.

WM. SMALLWOOD, Accountant,
20 and 24 Lombard St., Toronto.

While at Parry Sound I lost my diary, and have been unable to compare the accounts with the entry made at the depot.

The work along the lake was pursued during the summer with difficulties by reason of the depression in business, also from a lack of a sufficient supply of scriptures, and from a lack of cash to meet expenses, and was obliged to borrow from some of the good friends to get started, also by the delay and non-arrival of supplies forwarded, and from other embarrasments.

I started from Midland round the Georgian Bay northward, it being 15 years since last I labored in some of the places. I went also north to Webbwood, and west to Sault Ste. Marie, found men of many nationalities working upon the canal, and some that I had no scriptures for. I also did a little upon the Michigan shore, and upon St. Joseph's Island and Manitoulin Island. The Ojibway Indian Scripture Reader published by the mission last summer I found very acceptable among the Indians, one Indian lad giving his last 50c. for an English Bible, a hymn book and reader in Indian and English; another who paid me about $2 for Indian books, to whom I said, "You are not good Indian, you drink too much whiskey," having seen him on a past occasion intoxicated, to which he said he was very weak, but he loved Jesus and stood to Him every time; it did not sound ill coming from an Indian 6 feet high. Some may be disposed to say that talk may do for an Indian, but not for intelligent, educated white men, but it would be well for all such to cultivate the thoughts of the poet who said:

Ashamed of Christ ! My soul disdains the mean, ungenerous thought,
Shall I deny the Lord, who has to men salvation brought;
But should we in the evil day from our professions fly,
The Lord before the assembled world the traitor will deny.

I have published for the use of the mission and the furtherance of the Lord's work during the year an Ojibway Indian and English Scripture reader, 1000 copies; a French Daily Text Book, 2000 copies; a French and English Scripture A B C Book, 5000 copies; and have an Ojibway and English of the same in hand, 4000 copies; also a French and English Scripture reader, 1000 copies; (a second edition) the first thousand having been used. These are necessary as the first steps in the ladder of Christian knowledge, but it is a lamentable fact that many who have a knowledge of letters, books and bibles, are far from knowing the Lord, who is set forth therein, who exercises loving kindness, judgment and righteousness in the earth, not owning him as their personal friend and Saviour. It may be truly said of many to-day, as Moses said long ago; they are children in whom is no faith; or, at least, no faith which works by love, or things would be very different among us to what they are. Some personal assistance was sought and obtained for the work, but has since been dispensed with, being deemed unprofitable.

I have been informed upon reliable authority that the trunk with the magic lantern and other goods belonging to the mission, which was lost by the officials of the Canadian Pacific Railway, was detained in one of the company's railway stations, and finally broken open by an official of theirs and the contents taken away. In the suit I obtained jury's judgment for $108, which the company found means to have set aside, saying there was not evidence that it came into their hands. My solicitor has written to them concerning the statement given to me of the contents of box taken from their premises, and the $400 justly due me in the loss and trouble and expense put to concerning it. They esteemed the solicitor's letter not worth noticing. The contents of the box were described to me so that I knew the statement to be correct. It is a marvel that such injustice can find shelter under the name of justice, and these haughty holders of wealth and power trample to death a poor man's right, and there is none to deliver. But the Lord has engaged to break the oppressor to pieces—Amen. Their glory is short and their judgment certain except they repent. I received also a statement from the Secretary of State concerning the petition put into the Dominion Government two years ago, asking for some assistance to pursue the work of instruction among the Indians and others, but was informed that the application could not be entertained.

ELEVENTH YEAR'S REPORT.

1894. The number of Scriptures aud Scriptural books supplied in the district by the mission during the past summer has been 1,340, in six languages. The cash received for those supplied there, including a few back payments, has been $163.76. Those given in whole or part amounted to $11.89. Also 1,296 have been supplied outside the district, which have been made note of, for which $102.94 has been received, and $22.94 worth have been given; also many hundreds of our published books have been given to contributors. The religious services were conducted in the district in various parts, and many also have been held outside the district in various parts, also at the rooms, 202 King Street, East, Toronto. Friends have conducted prayer and exhortatory services, which are growing in activity and usefulness, and are conducted daily, morning and evenings at 8 o'clock, and also at noon. Great blessing is anticipated in answer to fervent and continued supplication, thanksgiving and praise.

The united contributions of the year have been $1490.55, and the amount received by sales $266.76; disbursements, $2176.75; and the assets over liabilities, $905.60. The number of scriptures, scriptural and helpful books supplied in the district by the mission and missionary since 1892 has been 13,640 in 17 languages, and 618 religious services conducted; and the united contributions, $11,325.33. Also much work of a similar kind has been done outside the district, while 20 various editions of scriptural and rudimental books of instruction and tracts have been published by the mission and for its use, in 5 languages, and others are being published, numbering 44,000 copies already published. These have been freely used and found to be helpful.

H. GRANFIELD, Bookkeeper,
212 King St. East, Toronto, Ont.

The journey during the past year with the supplies was limited to Muskoka, Parry Sound, Georgian Bay, Nipissing and Sudbury Districts. The difficulty in making the sales to meet the various costs prevented me from going around Lake Superior which I was prepared to have done, having ample supplies but could not meet the cost, but on the journey there was pleasing evidence that the work was productive of the desired result of producing repentance toward God and faith in our Lord Jesus Christ.

I have endeavored to obtain from the C. P. R. Co., some redress for the grievous loss sustained in the work by their negligence. I have written them four letters. The following is the only reply received:

Canadian Pacific Railway Company.
Office of the Assistant General Manager,
Montreal, January 29, 1895.
Geo. Buskin, Esq., 202 King Street East, Toronto, Ont.

Dear Sir,—Replying to your letter of the 7th, I have made careful enquiry into your claim referred to therein, and find that you have no ground whatever for asking this Company to make good the loss of your box and contents, and I am surprised, therefore, at the statements which you make in your annual report.

Yours truly,
(Signed) THOS. TAIT, Assistant Gen'l Manager.

To which I sent the following reply:

202 King St. East, Toronto, Ont..
January 30th, 1895.
Mr. Thos. Tait,
Asst. Gen'l Manager, C.P.R., Montreal, Que.

Dear Sir,—Thanks for your acknowledgement to my letter, but it implies that I am a simpleton, fraud, or crazy. You may evade my just claim in what language you please.

The Almighty shall plead my case against you, and execute judgment for me. It might have been settled in the beginning for $50.

My Christian advice is, put things straight, or Heaven will straighten it, and the Company will suffer loss.

I have enclosed you the case in printed form.

I am, Dear Sir,
Yours truly and respectfully,
GEO. BUSKIN.

I am far from desirous of striving, but such unnecessary inconsideration by men of such great possessions is past endurance, and our consolation must be in the words of the Lord who has said that every tongue that shall rise up in judgment against you thou shalt overthrow; this is the heritage of the servants of the Lord. And their righteousness is of Me, saith the Lord.

TWELFTH YEAR'S REPORT.

1895. The number of Scriptures and Scripture books supplied in the district by the mission during the past summer have been 810 in six languages. The cash received for those supplied there, including a few back payments, has been $136.85. Those wholly given, or in part, have been valued at $11.38. Also 1,235 Scriptures and books have been supplied outside of Algoma district, for which $127.03 have been received, and $10.30 worth have been given. Hundreds of our published books have been left with the contributors, who in many cases have been well pleased to receive them. Religious services have been conducted in the district in various parts, as strength would permit. Similar services have been held outside the district. The rooms of the depot, 202 King Street East, Toronto, have been and are kept open from 8 a.m. to 9 p.m. daily. There have been indications of blessings from the prayer services here. Nothing that the world would call great has been accomplished, but indications are that the labor is not to be in vain in the Lord.

We would gladly have our numbers and capacity enlarged

and improved, yet whereunto by grace we have obtained we will walk by the same rule and mind the same things, and like Paul at Rome we receive all who come in to us, Acts 28:30.

There is need of enlarging our operations and usefulness, for which we have a fervency of desire, though our capacities are very limited. It may be made more effectual by the presence and hearty co-operation of all who love the Lord and His Word.

The united contributions for the year have been $1,467.88, and the amount received by sales, $263.88. Disbursements, $2,288.66. Liabilities, $1,464.40. Assets over liabilities, $400.39. The number of Scriptures, Scriptural and helpful books supplied in the district by the mission and the missionary since 1882 have been 14,450 in 17 languages, and 630 religious services conducted; and the united contribution, $12,793. Also much work of a similar kind has been done outside the district. Last year and this, 2,531 Scriptural books have been supplied. 21 various editions of Scriptural and rudimental books of instruction, and tracts, have been published by the mission for its use in five languages, numbering 59,000 copies already published. These have been freely used and found to be helpful.

WM. SMALLWOOD, Bookkeeper,
114 Church Street, Toronto.

Again our Ebenezer is raised in acknowledgment of God's merciful hand with us, in bringing us so far through the conflicts and difficulties of the work to the present time, and has engaged not to forsake us. In God's name we would thank the friends who have helped with us in the work, trusting that they also experience that in doing good to others they themselves are blessed.

Of the thousands of copies of the Holy Scriptures, in whole or part, which have been scattered in the district and out of it by the agency of the mission, some I know are doing their divinely appointed work of comfort and instruction and formation of godly character.

Some in their ignorance and wilfulness have asked me if Bibles are good for feeding horses and drawing saw-logs. Others said they have never read it; and some cannot read it, having never learned how. Some by priestly rule of terrorism are deluded from so doing; and some say there is no God, and will not believe His revelation to man. Others from poverty and care have not the Scriptures, and therefore cannot exercise themselves in its records. These are some of the many experiences I have had in this highly favored land, while there are many who rejoice in the knowledge and grace of God, and some who possess the means of grace and abuse it, or do not use it; but there are hundreds of millions beyond our limits, whose light is as darkness, they know not the living and true God, nor Jesus Christ whom He has sent. Vast multitudes, through the ignorance in them, are practically and professedly, and with combined effort laboring to put out the light of God's truth, and with demoniacal bitterness gnash their teeth in their work of murderous destruction and opposition which is now being carried out against the Armenian Christians. To us through these very people came long ago, "Be thou faithful unto death and I will give thee a crown of life." Rev. 2:10. Let us with them seek grace to be faithful. It becomes us all to be strong in the grace of our Lord Jesus Christ, that we may overcome the evil with the good, resisting the adversary, steadfast in the faith. The greater the evil, the greater the opportunity to evidence God's power and grace, through the Holy Spirit, to overcome seven times. Christ has given us this word, Rev. 2 and 3 chap., "Be not overcome of evil, but overcome evil with good." But sometimes the adversary comes as an angel of light, and his ministers as ministers of righteousness. With increased diligence let us strive to do the Master's work. For our encouragement he has said, "I am with you, and will not leave you."

The work during the past year was pursued among some of the islands of Lake Huron to Sault Ste. Marie, and then back to Sudbury and North Bay. I would like to have taken in Parry Sound and the railway, but with the income from what I supplied I conld not meet expenses, and there were so many places for the little I-had that I was obliged to halt in order to meet the demands for payment.

My son, who for two or three years had been desirous that I should extend my visit to the west of Lake Superior, (and I also was anxious so to do, but lacked the means,) I regret to say died on the 7th of October last from the discharge of his gun after returning from a little hunt, on the 4th day after the accident. His age was 28 years. Another evidence that in the day we look not for God, He may call us away. Be ye therefore ready.

It will be gratifying to many to see that the long-talked of Sault Ste. Marie Canal is completed after much labor. I have given in the past views of its construction work, so now I give a view of it completed, and with it a word concerning a little share I have had there in the past:

"Jan. 2, 1891. A mission Room has been opened for the laborers at Sault Ste. Marie Canal by Mr. George Buskin, who has labored constantly in the district since the construction of the Canadian Pacific Railway."---Pioneer.

The Presbyterian Church bought out my investment in it, and also the building, and they still had it operating when I was there last July. I also had the pleasure of supplying a few Scriptures and books among the laborers on the water power there, and held a few religious services. I trust that my labors in the Master's name, and my statement, may all be satisfactory to my helpers and friends; and if I have any adversaries, the least harm I wish them is, that they shall go and do likewise.

But while I am thankful for the favor I find for the Master's sake, I must in honesty say that I sometimes make many calls and find little favor. On occasions of late I made about 50 calls and received $1.00 and on another I kept an account of 50 calls and the answers received. One would think from their answers they were all bankrupt; my mind was made up to print the answers---meaning no offence, but like a looking glass, to show how unlike Christ in many cases is the name of Christian in these days---I received $1.50 but I cannot find the record I made, but it will turn up again for there are no failures of the sort where the heavenly records are kept, but had they invested $50,000 in Christ's work instead of $1.50 they would not have hurt themselves, for one of the least told me he had lost $70.000 during the year and his partner the same. A good Methodist brother a little time ago gave me a dollar for the work, saying he wished it was more. He had not long ago invested $5,000 in real estate, and it was all gone. Better, said he, I had given it to the Lord's work. We are bid to lay up treasure in heaven, and to make to ourselves friends of the mammon of unrighteousness--that is by manifesting the kindness of God to each other and helping those who cannot help themselves.

I have left out from the mission account the $330 which I should have recovered from the C.P.R. Co. for the loss and cost concerning the box with the magic lantern. To Mr. Thos. Tait, Assistant Gen'l Manager's statement in his letter, that I had no claim whatever on the Company, I append the following statement, the original of which is in their possession:

Duluth, South Shore and Atlantic Railroad,
Sault, Mich., Dec. 3, 1890.
To Mr. Evanson, station master, Sault Ste. Marie, Ont.:
"The bearer arrived here on the 29th November from Port Huron; he had a box checked to Sault, Mich. As he wished to go to Sault Ste. Marie, Ont., I took up his check and marked the box in several places 421. He now claims that this is not there. Can you kindly trace and see what has become of it? He stood by and saw me mark this box and helped put it on the train; it was not put off again. G. F. G."

This statement I received from the baggage man at the direction of the station master of the Union Station. This is the last station on the Sault Ste. Marie Branch of C. P. R. See their time tables and tickets.

They received the goods and allowed them to be lost, and they defy all justice in not restoring them or making them good. But there is a God that judgeth in the earth. Psalms 58:11.

THIRTEENTH YEAR'S REPORT.

1896. The number of Scriptures and Scriptural books, supplied in the district by agency of the mission during the past summer have been 629 in 6 languages. The cash received for those supplied there being $84.84. The value of those given there in whole or part, was $7.85. The number supplied by sale outside the district have been 709 for which have been received $78.06, many hundreds also of our published books have been left with the contributors, and in many cases paid for, and in some cases the price being entered among the contributions. Not much interest has been shown lately in the premises, 202 King St. E., Toronto. They have been again kept open from 8 a.m. till 9 p. m. daily. Most visitors come for temporalities and few for spiritual advantage. There are few to join us in prayer, and probably were we in China, India or the South Seas there might be found those who would company with us more numerous, and more desirous of the grace of God, that can be found in Him alone. $22 has been volunteered in aid of the Armenians from the notices which we have given concerning them, and others also have been reminded of their condition and in other ways have sent to their help. We are willing to do great things if it is possible in the Saviour's name, and if not we are content to do what we can and better we would do if we could. Not one dollar has been volunteered this year to sustain or further the work from our notices in the store window. All that has been received had to be personally sought for. No doubt the business depression has hindered many in the extent of their liberality, but if they more fully realized that the Lord is rich to all them that call upon Him in truth, there would be more diligence in seeking and serving Him, and more fellowship in His work, more joy in His service, more purpose in prayer.

Commencing the work at Mattawa and North Bay and then going south through Muskoka several times touching the Parry Sound Railroad and construction, I passed over ground that I had not visited for twenty years. Fields and homes and villages are there, which on my previous visits were solid bush. Though the times were very depressed, and money very scarce some took pleasure in the good news for God's kingdom and grace. But though God is calling with patience and love, bestowing His mercy and grace, the devil is busy with corruption and vice, hardening the hearts and blinding the mind with vanity, foolery, and lies, while the name of Christian religion oft is dragged in iniquitie's mire. The Master's whip of small cords if used again would serve a good cause in stopping this blot to His name and His laws. The following I copy from a handbill, marked with Christian degeneracy. I regret to waste the time and paper to print it,—it professes to serve Christ's cause, and raise money to build a rectory by sports and games.

Aug. 5, '96, at Trout Creek. Programme, bicycle race, hotel-keepers' race, three hundred yard race for old men, two hundred yard race for married men, two hundred yard race for boys under thirteen, two hundred yard race for girls under 12 years, five legged race for grown men, merchants' race, clerks' race, egg race, walking match for bachelors, walking match for ladies, spelling match for teachers, running hop step and jump, running long jump, four hundred yard walking match, Liberals vs. Conservatives, open to all Scottish highland dance, prize for prettiest baby eighteen months and under, prize for homeliest man on the ground, prize for homeliest woman on the ground, tug of war North Bay vs. Burk's Falls,&c., &c. Eloquent Orators from the Queen City at 4.30 p. m. to deliver addresses. Admission 25cts. Children 15cts. Supper 25cts. Soft drinks, refreshments, &c. This is to build a recory. To the rector I addressed the following letter:—

Dear Sir,—   BRACEBRIDGE, ONT., Aug. 4th, 1896.

I have respectfully to state to you that your announced pic-

nic in the aspect of your profession is an ungodlike piece of business. Paul the apostle reminds us of the transgression and judgment of those who eat and drink and rise up to play. The Lord who is no respecter of persons will not pass by your ungodliness in this matter unless you repent and put it away.
Dear Sir, yours truly,
G. BUSKIN.

These things look like Satan's caricature of the good Shepherd and His sheep,---such religious pastors and leaders had better pursue some honest and useful calling than disgrace and corrupt the profession of the glorious gospel of the blessed God by such vile trickery and godlessness. And in this the old saying is quite true, "One fool makes many," and to be fooled out of the inheritance of the Kingdom of God because of unrighteousness is the greatest of all folly and will bring endless lamentation and irrecoverable loss.

The following is inserted and copied from the "North Bay Times," Thursday, July 23rd, 1896:

ABUSE AND PROFANITY.

Editor The North Bay Times:

Dear Sir,--Will you please favor me by giving publicity to the following, as it may be profitable for the future. On Saturday evening last between 7 and 8 o'clock, at the corner of the post office, while endeavoring to set forth the glorious character of our blessed Saviour as declared to us in the Holy Scripture in Psalm 72. I received prolonged abuse from a man whose conduct was more that of a lunatic from Bedlam than a sane person, which afforded great glee to a number of persons gathered round, both young and old, and though I sought his name or someone to witness against him concerning his abuse and profanity, there was no one to help shame such corruption or show respect to the speaker. When a Christian man occupied in a work of practical Christian benevolence can be reviled upon the public streets and repeatedly called a d--n fraud, and no man would witness against such lawless wicked conduct, things must be fallen low in North Bay, and Christian life needs reviving. Apart from Bible teaching the law provides that any person disturbing a religious assembly can be sent straight to jail by the order of a magistrate present, and the law is also against profanity and abuse. I have been occupied constantly for more than 12 years in circulating the Holy Scriptures and Christian literature over many hundred miles of the country, and when a man or any company of men can turn the declarations of God's Word into ridicule if there be no law or order to shame such conduct, the God of heaven will recompense it with shame and everlasting contempt on their heads unless they change their conduct. I afterwards saw the same man assail in a similar manner the Salvation Army women while they were occupied in speaking, but he was driven away by the hotel keeper. GEO. BUSKIN.

Algoma Colportage Mission, 202 King St. E., Toronto.

A great trouble was experienced by us. Last May some person started a fire outside our premises, which destroyed some of our stock to the amount of $200 or more. At the time, I was waiting for the train to pursue my journey to North Bay. While waiting, I saw a statement in the paper, "Many Bibles in flames," which occasioned me immediately to return. We were much exposed by the long delay of repairing the premises which was not completed for about three months afterwards. For a time I felt bewildered, not knowing how to overcome the difficulties, having no insurance.

During the year several useful books have been published by the Mission, which will be helpful for the work, both in French and English, and others also are progressing in French and Indian. But heavy liabilities lie upon our hands, which makes our progress slow. And our creditors need their money. Nearly $1,200 are needed to discharge our obligations with the various houses that are helping us in the work, which will be seen by looking at our liabilities. We will leave the matter with the Lord and our brethren, while striving to the uttermost to do our duty.

During the year we have had several men volunteer for the work, two had not courage to start, and one was hindered by various home responsibilities. He proved himself the best of the numerous persons who have undertaken to help with us. But means are too slow to meet his necessities. He worked for five weeks, but at present there is fourteen dollars due to him for his labor. Self-seeking was no part of his exercise. His labor was for the extension of the grace and kingdom of the Lord. No doubt at some future time he will again be in the field.

The united contributions of the year have been $1,829.03. The amount received by sales, $169.90. Disbursements,

$1,991.93. Liabilities, $2,445.00. Assets over liabilities, $550.70. WM. SMALLWOOD, Bookkeeper, 136 Harbord Street, Toronto. The number of Scriptures and Scriptural books supplied in the district since 1882 have been 15,073, in 17 languages, and 633 religious services held, accompanied with tract distributing. Also much work of a similar kind outside the district. During the past three years, 3,264 Scriptures and books have been supplied and taken account of, and a large number of religious services held. To the present time, 25 editions of elementary Scriptural books and tracts have been published by the Mission for its work, numbering 80,000 copies in 5 languages, and two more are published, one in French, and another in Indian and English, at a cost of nearly $800, and all these are necessary for the work.

During the past year there has been published an Illustrated Anti-Profanity Card, to place in public places, to restrain corrupt expressions. Also, a French tract, "What think ye of Christ?" is the subject. The French and English daily text book is also completed. It is Educational and Godly in its character, being a literal translation of the King James Version into the French language. There is also an edition of the Gospel of Matthew being published in the English and (Ojibway) Indian with a history of the translations of the Holy Scripture into the English language printed in both languages. The Indians need such help, as well as white people, otherwise heathen traditions remain festering in their minds and hinder them from making progress in Christian character and knowledge. I know it will afford them both pleasure and profit, the same I have seen from the three former editions that have been printed for them by the Mission, for ten years I have been seeking opportunity to accomplish it. $250 is necessary to meet the cost before it will be completed.

Also I am thankful to say that by the hearty assistance of a good brother and other friends in Montreal, the Foxe's Book of Martyrs in French is now ready for the press. $500 is necessary to complete the payment of its publishing. It will be sold at 15 cents a copy, having 200 pages.

I now relate some facts concerning the difficulty of raising money for practical Christian work, and leave heaven and earth to judge.

The good brother who volunteered to help me in the work, I sent to collect funds to pay the various houses from whom our supplies haJ been obtained. He visited 23 towns. His railway fares alone cost $14.75, his board cost $28, his wages amounted to $33 for as many days at work; total costs, $80.75. From the 23 towns he received in free gifts to help the Northwest Mission, $29.75, which was $51 less than the amount expended to get it. On the way he supplied 190 Scriptures and books, and received for them $16.43, which was not more than cost, and those that were given, including circulars and tracts, would be a cost of nearly $5 more. His daily expenses were $2.40, and he received 90c. to meet it and help our good work's account. The books will certify what is here stated. This matter can speak for itself, and if all other servants of Christ fare as did our good brother, there is no wonder that little is accomplished in conversion.

FOURTEENTH YEAR'S REPORT.

1897. The past year has been attended with so many difficulties, that it has been impossible personally to pursue the work during the year in the district. At times greatly perplexed to find means to meet the various payments due to creditors. But through God's mercy more has been accomplished this year than in any former one, having utilized the services of others, besides what has been accomplished outside the district.

SAMPLE.

The following is a statement from one of our former contributors, who has for some years resided in Alberta:—"The people are unable to buy supplies. A few cheap Bibles would be very acceptable; also the illustrated sheets of the primary department, old and new Sabbath School papers, also magazines suitable for reading room for the young men of the neighborhood, who frequent dances for want of a better place." To whom I sent two cases of 100 lbs. each, of new and second-hand matter as requested. The new books of the first case were, 12 Bibles, 12 Testaments, 6 large Testaments and Psalms, 2 smaller ones, 20 Hymn Books and music, 12 Annals of the Poor, 2 Cree Testaments, 2 Voices from the Orient, 12 books, viz.: Pilgrim's Progress, Evidences of Christianity and Walks About Zion, 6 Watts' Children's Hymns, 50 Scripture A B C, 25 Easy Readers, value $22, besides Sunday School matter, tracts and magazines. Our friend being an active Christian worker, they were well placed and duly acknowledged.

There has been sent into the district for the work, 8 packing cases of 100 lbs. each, filled with reading matter, namely:

Scripture tracts, magazines, &c; five cases for the camps and three for general use. 21,000 books have been published this year for the work, in Ojibway (Indian), French and English, and 15,000 tracts in French and English have also been printed.

To meet the cost of the various operations of the work, 84 towns have been visited, $1745.31 in all received (and some books, Scripture tracts and magazines). $56.92 of this amount was contributed at 21 various religious services and associations; the balance of the contributions was received from over 1,800 various contributors, and five times that number of persons have been called upon in order to obtain it. We leave this statement for the reflection of our friends and readers. In a multitude of cases, of congregations and persons, I am confronted with the statement of the great things that are being done, and yet, in the City of Boston, Mass., in 9 days I received cash $1.10 and a donation of tracts.

The work summarized is as follows: 796 Scriptures and books to the district for general use, value $82.85. Scriptures and books for shanties given, 259, value $19; no money as yet has been received for these books. Together these are 1,055, value $101.85. Also those sold and paid for number 1,099. Received in payment for them, $121.83. 524 have otherwise been supplied, for which we expect to receive $25.10. The total number supplied by sale and gift has been 2,769, the total value if paid for is $248.78. Also a large number of the published stock of the Mission has been donated to the contributors. This makes the total supply for the laborers and the district since the commencement of the Mission to be 16,128, in 18 languages. Also many thousands of tracts and magazines continue to be distributed. 4,363 Scriptural books in several languages have been supplied outside the district, and accounted for. The united contributions since 1884 for the work have been $16,-428.24. The number of religious services conducted in the district stands as last year, 630, but many have been held in other parts of the land.

The united contributions for the year were $1867.14; the Disbursements were $1867.14; the Assets are $2,980; the Liabilities are $1,906.05; Assets over Liabilities, $1,073.95.

WM. SMALLWOOD, Accountant,
136 Harbord St., Toronto.

The results of the work give undeniable evidence that the Lord takes part with them that fear Him, and by faith in Him

A scene on the Soo Canal.

A scene on the Soo Canal.

can say, "I shall not die, but live, and declare the praise of the Lord;" "And though I walk in the midst of trouble, He will revive me, and compass me about with songs of deliverance."

Gratefully acknowledging the kind help of our friends; desiring that grace, mercy, peace and plenteous goodness may be with all them that love our Lord Jesus Christ; asking also to be sustained by your prayers.

Yours in the hope of the Gospel,
GEORGE BUSKIN.

FIFTEENTH YEAR'S REPORT.

1898. Through God's mercy we are permitted once more to record the events connected with our work, ending with Dec. 1898, and to enter upon another year in the labor connected with God's service, having gratefully to record His condescending grace and care, and thankfully acknowledge the fellowship and assistance of our helpers and friends and brethren in Christ in the work, and rejoice in the measure of God's grace so widely bestowed.

The difficulties of our pathway may be judged by the following: In four different towns and places have we been obliged to borrow money to get to another place; and in another to leave a portion of board unpaid, the liberality and hospitality in God's service being of such a meagre character; and failing to find the necessities for the work, endeavored in vain to borrow sufficient to pay the cheap rates to the Pacific coast, and then work back, supplying the Bible and books now in stock for the work.

A synopsis of the work is as follows: 645 Scriptures and books have been supplied during the year, in the Algoma district, in several languages. The money received for the same being $99.63. The books given away there, value $5.80, besides tracts and magazines. Number supplied outside the district being 1,076. Total amount received for them, $82.86. This includes the payment for some supplied last year, still leaving some unpaid for. Those given for camps and otherwise during the year, we value $14. Those given to contributors to the good work are not included in these. The total supplied by the Mission for Algoma and the North-West have been 16,773 Scriptures and books in 18 languages. Large quantities of tracts and magazines continue to be distributed. The number of Scriptural books supplied outside the district, and not numbered previously, as far as account of them has been kept, are

5,441, in 5 or 6 languages. Together they numbered 22,214. These have been at various prices from 5c each to $15, all being of a practical Christian character.

The united contributions for the work since 1884 have been $18,163.23. A few religious services have this year been conducted while travelling in the Algoma district and other parts, as strength and opportunity allowed. We bless God for what has been done, and our friends will please accept our unfeigned thanks for the help rendered, though it would have afforded much joy to have accomplished more; but by God's grace and mercy will continue the work as it has already been done, in dependence upon God and the good will of His servants, through the name of our common Saviour, reminding our friends of the need of their prayers as well as their substance, so as to cause the work to redound to God's honor and men's salvation.

The united contributions for the year were $1,917.51; the disbursements, $1,917.51; the assets, $3,190; the liabilities, $1,950.03; assets over liabilities, $1,139.97.

WM. SMALLWOOD, Accountant,
136 Harbord St., Toronto.

NOT ALL SMOOTH SAILING.

The course of true love does not always run smoothly as may be seen from the following:

Brockville, Ont., March 16th, 1898.
To the Committee of the Religious Tract Society,
102 Yonge St., Toronto, Ont.
Gentlemen :

Appended to this statement is a letter which I addressed to you on May 16th, 1897, per Mr. J. K. Macdonald, whom I now understand to be president, to which letter from whatever cause, I have received no answer, which as a man and a Christian I am entitled to. Gentlemen, I believe in a personal God, the rewarder of those who serve Him, the rebuker of those who despise Him, though He bears long with rebellion; and further, I esteem the Holy Scripture to be His authoritative command to all His creatures, from which none are excused or can escape its sentence, and more especially responsible are all those who call Jesus Lord; they have a moral obligation to attend to the least of His commands, and marvellous that it should be necessary to make such statements to men of such high cultivation, official capacity and abundant Christian profession. "We do well to search and try our ways and turn again to God." The occasion of sending to you now is, the continuance of the work of mischief complained of in my former letter (which I append and send again). From town to town I have to learn of the petty mischievous insinuations and statements of your agent against me—saying that my work is an intrusion upon the limits of your Society and that the books I have published are unnecessary and can be obtained from your depot, which is untrue, (with one exception). A firm in London, Eng., to whom I sent and from whom your Society purchased supplies, offered to furnish me with a stock of them for cash, which I had not on hand to pay. I had 3000 copies printed in Toronto to save me again begging business favor and being refused. Also your agent has given the impression to some who have assisted me in the work, that he was acting in my place. You and your agents should do all the good you can, but don't do evil that good may come, for if you sow evil seed it will bear evil fruit and when carried home will be a heap of grief. I would ask where were your agents at work in the district in 1875 to '78 when I labored in the Gospel through large districts of Muskoka, Parry Sound, and the Georgian Bay among mill-men, shanties, railway-men and settlers, not for hire or reward, and then came to Toronto, not of my own will, to seek organized help to continue and enlarge the work begun, and sought it in vain? And yet I was known, having held open air gospel preaching through the streets of Toronto from the Don Bridge to the Queen's Park, and public prayer services in the Park at 7 o'clock Sunday mornings and at other hours till evening. These services have been sustained at intervals in various ways and places from 1874 till now, my door in Toronto being open continually to all who come in Christ's name. Where were your agents or agent in the Thunder Bay district in 1882-3-4-5, when I travelled there, hundreds of miles, supplying Scriptures and conducting religious services? Would the people have bought thousands of copies from me if your agents had supplied them all they needed? Other agents I have met but only one of yours, at Coldwater, about 110 miles north of Toronto. The occasion of my returning that way was from being unwell. This was about two years ago. I know that in 1884 your late secretary offered me the sum of $300 per annum to do work of the kind there for your Society at a time when the commonest board there was $5 a week, $2 a day for transients, or 50c a meal, which proposal I regarded as heartless ignorance, to say the least of it. I answered, "And starve my wife and children," and with unceremonious unkindness they left me to myself. But a week later after my advertising my errand to Toronto, coming from beyond Sudbury, your secretary candidly said the Society was not in a position to sustain it, for they could not sustain what work they had in hand. Twelve months later at the request of one of your contributors, your secretary gave me a note saying I was doing a *bona fide* work, and much good would doubtless result from it, knowing the supplies that had been sent to me in the districts from your warehouse, the costs of which I paid, except for some leaflets, and not any donation of cash has ever come from your Society to meet the cost of my work.

I hope this will be the last of this babbling and mischief making. Your men have compelled me to turn up this matter, which I would gladly leave buried, but if you want to keep it going you have yourselves to please, but in doing so the more the disgrace. Be assured that God who judgeth righteously will maintain the right of the poor against those who rise up against them, and He will not forsake me of His mercy. The conduct of your agents practically vilifies the score or more persons who have kindly certified to the character of my labors and also asserts that my statements of travels and sales, and my years of residence there are a delusion. Alas ! what simpletons men will make of themselves to gratify their ungodly whims and vanity. Your account books show the amount of goods bought and paid for by me and sent to Port Arthur, Sault Ste. Marie, Algoma Mills and elsewhere. I respectfully ask what reasonable persons can think of such professed Christian conduct, and worst of all, what will the Lord think of it, who is of purer eyes than to behold iniquity ? You have seen me journey with my stock of Bibles and books upon the lake, and they have been inspected by you. You have also heard my exhortation on the boat, from Isaiah 54:17. "Every tongue that riseth in judgment against thee thou shalt condemn. This is the heritage of the servants of the Lord and their righteousness is of me saith the Lord." Religious paper and ink and talk goes for very little unless God's Holy Spirit has made us to be "the living epistles of Christ, that can be known and read of all men." It is still true to-day as said by our Lord, "If they have called the master of the house Beelzebub, how much more they of his household." The end of all such wordiness will soon be to be "cast out and trodden under foot of men." The sooner there be a thorough purging of this corruption, the better, so that in truth we may learn to love our enemies and not abuse our friends. We are Christ's friends if we do what He commands us, and among them he says, "if thy brother trespass against thee rebuke him, and if he repent forgive him." The counsel of Gamaliel will not be out of place at the present: "Refrain and let alone, if this work be of man it will come to nought, but if of God, ye cannot overthrow it, lest haply ye be found even to fight against God."

Yours in the service of Christ,
GEO. BUSKIN,
202 King St. E., Toronto, Ont.

[Former letter addressed to care of Mr. J. K. Macdonald, as Hon. Secretary Religious Tract Society, 102 Yonge St., Toronto, Ont.]

Arnprior, Ont., May 16, 1897.
To the Committee of the Religious Tract Society,
Toronto, Ont.
Gentlemen :

I respectfully request that you will do me the justice to direct your secretary and travelling agents to cease their intimations to those on whom they call that I am a sort of renegade from your Society. When spoken with they may possibly deny doing so, but since your late secretary joined to warn the public against me in the Montreal Witness appending his name and the Society's thereto in 1885, thereby prejudicing the public mind against me (the effect of which is still lingering with some) thereby hindering me in the discharge of my debts due to your Society and others. From then till this very time, extending from Sault Ste. Marie to Ottawa and from this place to Windsor and Sarnia, I have had to contend against the prejudice instilled by your servants in the minds of many concerning myself and the work I am engaged in, and even in your own offices whereby Mr. Harvey, Bible Society Secretary, reproached me a few days ago concerning reports from the "Soo," emanating from your secretary—and Mr. Duncan, Presbyterian minister—which I also heard there two years ago; Mr. Harvey also saying I am publishing false statements.

Gentlemen, I am not your Society's servant nor ever have been, though I may possibly be in some measure to individuals of your committee who personally have made donations to help forward God's work in my hands. The work of Christ is not as rival trade unions. Your servants should have enough to do to carry on the work of your Society without gossiping and scandalizing and hindering me in the Master's work. If personally I have done any person wrong let him make me acquainted with it in any way he thinks best and I will try and put things right, but slander does good to no one. Christ made himself of no reputation. Paul was satisfied to be as the offscouring of all things, and humility will pay best in the end. I think it is due to me that I should know from you that a proper admonition has been given to them, that at least the mischief already done should go no farther. My reports are facts and should inspire confidence and respect, and God's word and work is as free to me as to any other creature.

It is no gratifying work to me to send again this statement, but duty demands it. The rest I leave to the Almighty God, whose I am and whom I serve. This I can thankfully and humbly say.

    Gentlemen, yours truly in Christ's work,

            GEO. BUSKIN,
         202 King St. E., Toronto, Ont.

Concluding Remarks.

In the preceding pages there has been set before the reader, in a somewhat brief, imperfect, and incomplete form, (but may in the future be improved), some of the experiences of a Christian, who in simplicity and sincerity has sought persistently to pursue a pathway of obedience to Christ as made known in the Holy Scriptures, apart from the undue influences of human dogmatism, and yet seeking fellowship of all who sincerely make mention of the name of Jesus Christ as their only Lord and Saviour. It gives evidence of the discouragements and conflicts of the pathway. But contrasting the experiences and surroundings of '55 to '60 with that of '95 to '98, it can be seen in some measure at least, what the Lord has wrought through a servant so weak. It is evident that in some cases the enemy has plowed hard upon his back and made long his furrows, yet he has not prevailed against him, and also that bread and water according to the divine promise have been sure; and strength has been given according to the day, though no man's gold, or silver, or apparel has been coveted.

The Lord has loaded us daily with His benefits so that in truth it can be said, "Bless the Lord, Oh my soul and all that is within me bless His holy name." Another promise has been made good. His own hands also have been sufficient for Him, and the Lord has been a defence for us from our enemies. The Lord also has given many friends who have shown timely aid although not being favored much in the groves of denominational elevation, nor did we desire it much; and what need when prayer has long been made, "O Lord, let them that love thy name be as the sun which goeth forth in His strength." It is well to do our little for Christ's sake only. The failures in Christ's cause largely result from not being subject to the Holy Spirit and the Word of God; too often accepting the counsels and commandments of men and the human heart instead, so that there is but little fellowship of the Spirit, which implies love unfeigned and likeness to Jesus Christ. The Holy Spirit being given without measure to Him was His power for service. As the Scripture says, "The Spirit of the Lord God is upon me, because He hath anointed me to preach the Gospel to the poor, to heal the broken hearted, to preach deliverance to the captives and recovering of sight to the blind, and to set at liberty them that are bruised, and to preach the acceptable year of the Lord. Through the Holy Spirit He gave commandment to the Apostles whom He had chosen.

Men to-day look too much to the work of their own hands, their schools, colleges, and combinations, and too little to Jesus Christ. Few practically take their pattern from Him. Like parrots they may learn to talk and sing about Him and pray to Him, but in many cases it is doubtless true as the Lord said, "Though they make many prayers, I will not hear. Your hands are defiled." His counsel to "Wash and make you clean and put away the evil of your doing from before mine eyes; cease to do evil, learn to do well" is neglected. It is not enough to say well, but we must work in line with God, relieve the oppressed, judge the fatherless, and care for the widow, otherwise the solemn meeting is but iniquity. Climbing the ladder of knowledge is a dangerous exercise, for we are told that knowledge puffeth up—a sort of wind bag character—but charity edifieth, or grace which teaches us to take upon us the afflictions of the afflicted, as our Lord or the Apostle Paul did. Paul said, "Who is weak and I am not weak, or who is offended and I burn not?"

I trust that by God's blessing this record of more than forty years in the service of Christ may be the means of encouraging many young persons to cleave to Christ and His Word.

The Holy Scriptures are given us that the man of God may be perfected, throughly furnished unto every good work. Need we more when our Christ is the head over all principalities and powers, not only of this world but of that which is to come? The law of His mouth is better for us than thousands of Gold and silver. I counsel all both from His Word and from personal experience, Cleave to Christ and His Word. Do not barter it for profession, position, princes, principalities, the world, the flesh, or the devil.

Think of Moses who forsook Egypt, not fearing the wrath of the king. Though he suffered much, yet his gain was great and eternal. Of David with his shepherd's bag, sling, and stones, who assailed the vaunting Philistine giant. Of Daniel and his three companions in Babylon who refused the king's commandment, to bow down to the colossal and magnificent golden image, undaunted by the terrors of the fiery furnace. Of the Master Himself who set his face to go to Jerusalem and said, I must walk to-day and to-morrow and the day following, to the place of His suffering and death, of which city He said, "Thou that killest the prophets and stonest them that are sent to thee, how oft would I have gathered thy children together as a hen gathereth her brood under her wings, but ye would not." There he gave His back to the smiter and His cheek to them that plucked off the hair. There He looked for some to take pity and for comforters, and found none. There He poured out His soul unto death and was numbered with the transgressors, and bore the sins of many, and made intercession for the transgressors, crying, Father forgive them, for they know not what they do.

Then again we have the record of Paul the Apostle who says to us, "Be ye followers of me, even as I also am of Christ." Immediately upon his conversion Ananias, by the will of God ministered unto Him. Then Paul straightway preached Christ in the synagogue, proving that He is the Son of God. Here we may also learn a lesson from Ananias; when the Lord called him, he answered, "Behold I am here, Lord." He was told to go and enquire in the street named straight for Saul of Tarsus, "for behold he prayeth." It was an urgent matter. Saul the infant child of the kingdom was crying. His need must be attended to. Ananias began to debate; but there was no time to spare, he was to go at once, and so he did, and Saul was straightway filled with the Holy Ghost.

Obedience is better than sacrifice, and to hearken than the

fat of rams. Hearken to the voice of God by His Spirit and by His Word. The service may be small, but the results may be great. Does He say, Wash and be clean, in the fountain opened for sin and uncleanness? then do so. Does He say, Feed my sheep and feed my lambs? then do so. If thy resources be no more than that of the widow of Sarepta, deal it out and thou shalt find more. The five barley loaves and the two fishes among the multitude in the hand of Christ there shall increase so that there will be enough for all, and abundance left for future need.

But some may say, Times have changed and things are not to-day as they once were. Remember, Jesus Christ is the same yesterday, to-day and forever. The same for me and the same for you, and the same for all who shall come after us.

"Set thou thy hope in God,
In duty's path go on;
Fix on His Word thy sure repose,
So shall thy work be done."

Make no league with the inhabitants of the land, is God's admonition to His people. Blind unbelief is sure to err, but the Word of the Lord liveth and abideth forever.

There are three things for the believer to do. Look to Christ, His Word, and His service. And there are three things to be remembered for profit : Not to trust in the arm of flesh, nor in any son of man, for they will utterly supplant ; and he that trusteth in his own heart is a fool. If we cannot trust our own heart, we may not trust another's. But we are told to trust in the Lord with all our might and lean not to our own understanding. "In all thy ways acknowledge Him and He shall direct thy path." This must be a daily, hourly, and continual exercise until we arrive where David exclaimed, "The prayers of David the son of Jesse are ended," and that is in anticipation of the whole earth being filled with the glory of God. Psalm 72:19, 20. In Christ we shall keep clear of the fashionable runs of religiousness which may run the life out of us. Have faith in God and keep at His work, and all will be well. The harvest is still great and the laborers few, especially in the line I have pursued which has only been the pathway of Christian duty.

During the period of more than forty years have I not found a man who would steadfastly pursue it with me. Some have promised but failed to fulfil. Some have started, but could not stand for long. Of women, in justice to my deceased wife, I must say she was the most self-sacrificing and sincere.

To one who sometime since came and said, The work you are engaged in is what I would like to pursue. I said, You are the sort of man I would like to have, and if you feel like it, come along. But I must give you the words that Jesus gave to the man who said, I will follow thee whithersoever thou goest, to which the Master said, "Foxes have holes, birds of the air have nests, but the Son of Man hath not where to lay his head." But he would have fared no worse than the rest who left all and followed Jesus. His promise must be fulfilled, Seek first the Kingdom of God and His righteousness, and the needful things shall be added thereunto.

My only regret is that I had not more faith, understanding, and purpose in my earlier days, to have fought the good fight against the opposing forces of the world, the flesh and the devil. But the same grace, faith and purpose are daily needed and at the present time as in any time in the past. The promise is to those who are faithful unto death. The world, sin and ignorance require the service and devotion at the present as in any time in the past. Who is willing for Christ's sake and in His name to undertake the duty of His loving service for men's salvation and blessing? We must cast aside the works of darkness whether they be religious or irreligious, and put on the armour of light. Some persons think it is sufficient to be sincerely religious, no matter what its principles, but there is only one way to life, not many. Christ only is the Way, the Truth, and the Life. No man cometh to the Father but by Him. Then the evidence is given to us: Hereby we know that we have passed from death unto life, because we love the brethren, and because we love God and keep His commandments. Then there is another evidence: By His Spirit He has given us. The Spirit is to us, wisdom, power, love, and of a sound mind, whatever our deceitful hearts or any one else may have to say concerning us. Our mistakes and weaknesses are caused by reason of our failure to keep our eyes upon the Lord and His Word, and also in failing to earnestly seek to obtain His favor by prayer and supplication.

I pray the Lord to add His blessing to this testimony to His grace and goodness, and to strengthen weak hands, and confirm feeble knees, and may His servants increasingly realize that our God reigneth, and so be encouraged to trust Him and not be afraid in the midst of the darkness and discouragement of the present day. May the number of His elect be speedily gathered in, and may these few pages be as a light to those who sit in the region and shadow of death, and may they enter the ark of safety while there is room.

To all who find fault with our labor, I counsel them to do better if they can, for the Master will hold them responsible. To those who in the past have been our friends and helpers we wish them much grace and mercy before God, and trust the plainness of our record and utterances will be no offence. We are admonished to suffer the word of exhortation.

I desire the reader to understand that I do not seek the favor or frowns of any. I have simply written facts as they have occurred for the profit and instruction of all, without bitterness or prejudice to any.

To our friends or foes, and to all men we say, Peace and mercy be with you through the knowledge of Jesus Christ.
GEO. BUSKIN,
Toronto, Ont.; Rochester, N. Y.
March, 1899.

Testimonials.

Collection of reliable testimonials concerning the International Gospel and Colportage Mission from 1884 to 1898.

Port Arthur, July 22, 1884.
Mr. George Buskin has visited Port Arthur several times, holding in and out-door services faithfully and frequently as time permitted him, and practically useful too, as far as I can judge. His services at the jail are very acceptable, his addresses and appeals earnest and close. I can only add my expression of confidence in him, as well as in his work, and trust that in this, as well as in this colportage, he may be much blest.
JOHN F. CLARKE,
Sheriff.

194 College St., Toronto, Dec. 10th, 1884.
During my visit to the North-West last summer I had the pleasure of seeing Mr. Buskin. He was engaged in open-air preaching and colportage work, and I believe is doing much good. S. A. DYKE,
Pastor College St. Baptist Church.

Trinity College, Toronto, Dec. 10th, 1884.
I hereby certify that whilst doing missionary work along the line of C. P. Railway I frequently met Mr. Buskin, who was engaged in holding services among the men and distributing tracts and Bibles—evidently doing a good Christian work.
E. A. OLIVER,
Divinity Student.

Standard Pub. Co., 117 Yonge St., Toronto, May 5, 1885.
To Mr. N. Macintosh, Montreal:
Dear Sir,—At the request of Mr. G. Buskin, I send you a general statement of his account with our company. Since my management he has purchased $110.84 of Bibles and religious books, on which he owes a balance of $26.23, he has generally remitted instalments of larger and smaller sums. So far his transactions with us have been honorable, and we have no ground of complaint against him. Your truly,
G. RICHARDSON.

Extract from St. Catharines daily paper, Feb. 6th, 1885, endorsed by REV. M. PORTER:
Mr. Buskin, whose Christian Mission among the C. P. R. has been so favorably spoken of by the Toronto and Hamilton papers, and by persons conversant with it, is in the city collecting funds for this work, and from our personal knowledge and information of him and his work, we bespeak for him the kindly consideration of the public.

Sault St. Marie, Algoma, Dec. 3rd, 1885.
This certifies that we have known Mr. George Buskin for a short time, and believe him to be an earnest and sincere Christian. The work in which he is engaged is, in our opinion, a necessary work, viz., visiting the lumber camps, mills, and mining camps, and also the poorer classes of the newly organized Townships, supplying them with religious literature.
N. A. McDIARMID,
Methodist Minister.

A Returning Missionary.—Rev. Mr. Buskin, the Canadian Pacific Missionary, will return to the city in a few days, and will begin a series of street sermons. The Algoma "Pioneer" has the following to say of him: "Sault Ste. Marie cannot boast of having a Salvation Army and barracks, but it has a good strong-lunged street preacher, who holds forth every Sunday morning at nine o'clock; and thereby draws some sleepy people out of bed an hour or two sooner than usual. Keep at it, Mr. Buskin, and by and by perhaps it will be possible to see a decent-sized congregation in one of our three Protestant churches at 11 a.m."

MONTREAL HERALD, May 7th, 1886.

Algoma and North-West Evangelical and Scriptural Colportage Mission—G. Buskin, Missionary.

Toronto, May 12th, 1886.
252 Yonge St., Toronto, and Sault Ste. Marie, Ont.

To confirm the statement made in City papers, and that its debt of $85.95 may be removed, and a new supply of Scriptures, etc., furnished, a few friends kindly annex their names.

We, the undersigned residents of the city, being helpers to the Mission from its commencement, and some of us having a previous as well as present knowledge of the Missionary and his work, at his request, and for the encouragement of others to help the work, unite our testimony of confidence in his integrity and work.

(Signed) F. S. Robinson, Henry Pim, Thos. Woodhouse, H. B. Gordon, L. Duncan, William Davies, Wm. Davies, Jr., John Firstbrook, B. J. Hill, A. W. Mason, Aikenhead & Crombie. May 11th, 1886.

The Toronto Mail of December 6th, 1884, stated from my letter, concerning the summer's work: "Up to November 3rd, about 400 Bibles and Testaments have been supplied in eleven languages. Also 500 religious books and over 700 hymn books, with many thousands of religious tracts and magazines, and also sixty religious services held.

Y. M. C. A., Victoria Square, Montreal, July 14th, 1886.
Mr. Edmund J. Kennedy, Sec'y Exeter Hall, London, Eng.

Permit me to introduce the bearer, Mr. Buskin, who visits your city at this time. He is engaged in Christian work in the back districts of Canada, and would be glad to have the privilege of attendance at your rooms and meetings.

Yours faithfully, D. A. BUDGE,
Secretary.

The Religious Tract Society, 56 Paternoster Row,
London, Aug. 12th, 1886.
George Buskin c/o Mrs. E. Pavey, 35 Victoria St., Clifton, Bristol.

The Committee have much pleasure in voting you a supply of tracts in various languages, (12) for your interesting and important work in Canada. For languages not included in our grant it would be well for you to apply to the Toronto Tract Society.

With best wishes, I am faithfully yours,
SAMUEL GREEN.

British and Foreign Bible Society, 146 Queen Victoria St.,
London, E. C., Aug. 19th, 1886.
Mr. George Buskin, Dear Sir.

The Committee have responded to your application for a grant in aid of the Gospel Mission, which you are carrying on among Canadian Pacific Railway men, etc., by a grant of 300 Gospel portions, subject to the approval of our Auxiliary in Toronto, the Upper Canada Bible Society. If you will kindly call upon Mr. J. Harvie, the Secretary, on your return to Toronto, he will arrange with you as to the grant.

I am, dear Sir, yours truly, CHAS. FINCH.

(The grant referred to above has been received, consisting of 125 portions in 6 languages, 50 Testaments in 12 languages, and 2 Bibles, making about 14 languages.—G. B.)

From Mrs. C. H. Spurgeon,
Westwood, Upper Norwood, Aug. 9th, 1886.

Dear Sir,—You are not eligible for a grant from my book fund in the usual way, but I shall be very pleased to give you 250 of Mr. Spurgeon's sermons, if they can be distributed among those you labor for. If you take the enclosed note to Messrs. Passmore and Alabaston, 4 Paternoster Buildings, Paternoster Row, E. C., they will supply you with the number stated. Wishing you every success in your good work.

Believe me, truly yours,
(Mrs. C. H.) SUSIE SPURGEON.

The Sunday School Union kindly contributed £1.0.0 worth of small books and papers, more especially adapted for children.

Extract from "Algoma Pioneer," Oct. 8th, 1886.

Mr. Buskin, the street preacher, took his stand on Sunday,

morning and afternoon, and preached a sound Scriptural salvation doctrine. Good results must inevitably follow all faithful labor, no matter how uninviting the field, and this Gospel preacher will be no exception to the rule on the day when every man's work shall be tried of what sort it is.

Sault Ste. Marie, Mich., Nov. 15th, 1886.

This is to certify that George Buskin, Evangelical laborer and Colporteur, is in my estimation a very worthy brother and is doing a good work in the lumber camps and out of the way places as well as in the villages and towns; he has sold and given away large numbers of the Scriptures, besides Religious Books and Tracts. From what I have seen of him and his work, I heartily commend him to the confidence, the sympathy and the co-operation of all who love the name of the Lord Jesus.

JAMES GOODMAN,
Pastor of the Baptist Church.
(Who also will receive any aid on his behalf to further the work.)

Sault Ste. Marie, Ont.

I endorse the above statement willingly concerning Mr. Buskin and his work.—G. H. WHITNEY, Methodist Minister.

I heartily endorse this statement in regard to Mr. Buskin and his work.—J. A. McCLUNG, Methodist Minister.

I willingly endorse the above.

FRANK F. GREENE, English Church Minister.

Sault Ste. Marie, Ont., 13th July, 1887.

Mr. Geo. Buskin, well known in these parts as the Evangelical Missionary and Colporteur, is an earnest, zealous and successful worker for Christ. I say so from personal knowledge. I have been with him on his journeys, and seen him at work on his field, and have had him take part in certain services of my own, and on these occasions I have been pleased with his manner and the way he does his work. Evidently he has received the double baptism. Moreover I believe him to be an upright and honorable man in all his business transactions.

I therefore ask for my friend, Mr. Buskin, a welcome from all the good folks in the several churches, and hereby heartily commend him as a workman that needeth not to be ashamed, rightly dividing the word of life in his own sphere according to his ability, and as he has opportunity. Friends, help him.

E. B. ROGERS,
Presbyterian Minister, Sault Ste. Marie, Ont.

Rapids Railway and Bridge Camps, Sault Ste. Marie, Ont.
December 16th, 1887.

An expression of appreciation of the operations of the Algoma and North-West Gospel and Colportage Mission by the undersigned, who have been engaged, some for many months, in the construction of a portion of the Algoma Branch of the Canadian Pacific Railroad; also certifying that we have received many visits from the Missionary, Geo. Buskin, who has conducted religious services and supplied us with Scriptures and Scriptural books at easy prices, and distributed freely among us other religious literature.

Signed:
Contractors—R. G. Reid, per A. H. Bryson; A. H. Bryson, Paymaster, Sault Ste. Marie Bridge.
Workmen—Wm. Ross, J. S. Miller, Thos. Aikin, M. Thenault, D. M. Stewart, R. S. Butler, P. Cowly, Alexander Ross, Jas. Power, G. I. McKenzie, Thos. Galloway, Naughton McNaughton, J. F. Smith, John Samson, Geo. Wm. MacKenzie.

Accompanied with $4.50, a small subscription from a few men in the camp.

Echo Bay, Feb. 13th, 1889.

Some of the former confirmations have been:—From Echo Bay—James Stewart and Alex. Findlay; Stobie—Peter Stobie; Sucker Creek—Thomas Stickney; Algoma Mills—James Perry; Sudbury—Fred. and E. B. Eyre.

Sault Ste. Marie, Ont., Oct. 14th, 1890.

My Dear Sir,—You called on me a few days ago asking me if agreeable to grant you a testimonial as to the usefulness of the work in which you are engaged. I suppose you did so, as perhaps I am about the best able to testify to what you are doing, from the fact, that for more than four years I have been engaged in mission labors for our church in the parts where your work calls you. I can say that I have seen you in your field at your work, and watched your tact, your zeal and success, and I have found from personal enquiry that your labors of love for the Master have been blessed. I have learned, moreover, that your book sales and your good words spoken in your journeys have proved a blessing to souls. I have much pleasure therefore in renewing the former certificate I gave you, and hereby authorize you, should you see fit, for the good of the work in

One of the mills where Gospel Work was done.

One of the mills where Gospel Work was done.

which you are engaged, to read or show it to any of the friends of your mission. I am yours faithfully,
E. B. ROGERS,
Presbyterian Minister.

Spanish River, September 30, 1890.
I have frequently met with Mr. Geo. Buskin, and seen him engaged in his Colportage work in Algoma; he carries about with him an excellent assortment of religious books, which he sells cheap. He has books in English, French and Indian languages, the circulation of which is certainly fitted to do good both among the young and old. I heartily wish him success in the work of the Gospel.
JOHN RENNIE, Presbyterian Minister.

ALGOMA ADVOCATE, Thessalon, Sept. 26, 1890.
A Hard Worker.—George Buskin, of the Algoma Colportage Mission, has been making another visit among us in the operation of his work, being well loaded with supplies. The class of literature which is placed in the hands of our young men, who labor at times for months in our backwoods, as well as that placed in our homes, must awaken, cultivate and establish Christian character in those who peruse them; in addition to Bibles and Testaments in various languages, ranging from a few cents to a dollar or two each, he carries a large variety of other works; among his stock are seen Bible Companions, Bunyan's writings, Josephus' Jewish History, Church and Scripture History, in various forms; and a large variety of other excellent Christian matter. Mr. Buskin is a hard worker, in a good cause, and his friends here wish him Godspeed.

From Dr. Sullivan, Bishop of Algoma.
So far as Mr. Geo. Buskin's work consists in the distribution of copies of the Word of God in English, and other languages, in the district of Algoma, I desire to recommend it as worthy the support of all Christian people.
E. Algoma, Bishophurst, Sault Ste. Marie, Ont., Dec. 23, 1890.

DISTRICT NEWS, Jan. 2, 1891.—Two mission rooms have been opened at the Rapids, Sault Ste. Marie, for the use of the laborers on the canal: one under the charge of the Rev. F. Tapscott, of the Baptist Church, and the other by Mr. George

Buskin, who has labored constantly in the district since the construction of the Canadian Pacific Railway.—PIONEER.

Gore Bay, Manitoulin Island, Ont., Nov. 5, 1891.

This is to certify that the undersigned has great pleasure in testifying to the good work done by Mr. Geo. Buskin, Colporteur in the District of Algoma. The books and tracts are of a good and useful kind, and likely to result in much good.

J. H. McLEOD, Incumbent.

North Bay, Ont., Feb. 17th, 1892.

From what I know of Mr. Geo. Buskin, and the work in which he is engaged, I am able to add my testimony to the good he has done, and is doing, in a very necessitous and arduous field of Christian effort. In the circulation of the Scriptures and other good and wholesome books among those into whose hands they would not in all probability otherwise come, he is, I believe, accomplishing a valuable and much-needed work, in which I wish him continued and increasing success.

JAS. PULLAR, Presbyterian Minister.

Sturgeon Falls, Ont., Feb. 29th, 1892.

This is to certify that Mr. Geo. Buskin, of the Algoma Mission is doing a good work in the district. The books and tracts are of a good and useful kind, and likely to result in much good. He gave me a French Bible to give to a poor French woman that is too old to attend service in her own church. Her daughter told me the other day that her mother is reading it more or less all the time, and she says she will never be able to thank him enough for it. He also gave me some Indian hymns. I have given a few to some of the Indians; two were delighted with them. May God bless him in his work is the prayer of his friends,

E. H. AND S. B. EYRE.

SUDBURY JOURNAL, Sudbury, Ont., March 2, 1892.

Mr. George Buskin, of Algoma and North-west Gospel and Colportage Mission, will hold a meeting in the Presbyterian Church, on Friday evening, March 4, at 7.30 o'clock. Mr. Buskin has a large quantity of Bibles, tracts, etc., in various languages, which he sells very cheap.

January 30th, 1893.

I have known the bearer, Mr. George Buskin, for about 10 years. His work among the lumbermen and others in the northwest is worthy of the generous support of every Christian and every patriotic citizen. GEORGE STANLEY BURNFIELD,
Pastor North Presbyterian Church,
N. Sixth St., Philadelphia.

Philadelphia, Pa., 827 Wharton St., January 31st, 1893.

To Whom It May Concern:—From testimonials received regarding Mr. Buskin, I have no hesitation in recommending him and his cause to the liberal people of this city. He is a good and faithful missionary, who has done good work among the lumbermen in the woods. F. W. JOHNSON,
Pastor of Wharton St. Presbyterian Church.

Gore Bay, Sept. 1st, 1893.

This is to certify that I have looked over Mr. George Buskin's tracts and have very great pleasure in testifying to their general evangelical tone, and also to the good which he is doing for the Master in the district of Algoma.
J. H. McLEOD, Incumbent.

Rosseau, Ont., 30th July, 1894.

Mr. G. Buskin is an old friend of mine, and his work a good one, and he himself indefatigable in carrying it out. He has labored for years over a very wide and difficult field, as I can personally testify. GOWAN GILLMOR,
Incumbent (Church of England.)

St. Thomas, August 4th, 1894.

We believe brother G. Buskin is doing good work among the lumbermen and people of the northern part of Ontario. He is worthy of the generous support of the Christian people. Isa. 6:3; Rom. 8:28 (H). Yours in the Master's work,
HUNTER and CROSSLEY, Evangelists.

Sudbury, Sept. 6th, 1894.

Mr. Buskin's work among the lumbermen of this district has all my sympathies, and I believe it deserves the hearty support of all Christian people.
S. RONDEAU, Presbyterian Minister.

St. Luke's Rectory, Sault Ste. Marie, August 5, 1895.

This is to certify that I have known Mr. Buskin for the last twelve years. I have always admired and respected him as a faithful and indefatigable worker in the Lord's vineyard—engaged in a work of the utmost importance, that of spreading God's sacred truth among the dying masses of humanity. Truly God's Word shall not return unto Him void. Mr. Buskin should have the sympathy and help of all lovers of God and His blessed book. R. RENISON, Rural Dean of Algoma.

NORTH BAY TIMES, July 23rd, 1896.

Mr. Geo. Buskin, Missionary and Colporteur, visited the town for business. He attempted to speak on the post office corner on Saturday night, and while talking to a large gathering was accosted by a man who, after having a few words with him, called him a ——— villain. A man that would use such language on the streets should be promptly and severely dealt with.

August 4th, 1896.

This is to certify that in my judgment Mr. Buskin cannot fail to do good work by circulating among the lumbermen the books he carries with him. H. MOORE,

Meth. Minister, Bracebridge.

To Mr. Geo. Buskin, Lacombe, Alberta, March 10, 1897.

Dear Friend,—The first case sent by you came duly to hand, with $4.14 to pay. A quantity of the literature and all the picture rolls have been already distributed. One lot to a school in a needy district, the other to a school of an Indian orphanage. One of the Cree testaments I have already given away to an intelligent Cree Indian. The balance I may place in a needy district north-east of nere. I thank you very sincerely in the name of the Sabbath School Association for the assistance you and your Mission have rendered us. I regret that the freight practically took all the small balance in my hand for Sabbath School work. The second case came to hand a few days ago, with the same amount of charges. Our country is but sparsely settled as yet, and money is very scarce among the people. Praying that the blessing of the Master may be with you in your work. Yours very sincerely,

G. A. REED.

Spanish River, August 19, 1898.

These certify that the bearer, Mr. G. Buskin, of the International Evangelical and Colportage Mission of Algoma and the Northwest, is engaged in a good work. I have examined the books that he has for sale, and can heartily recommend them to the general public. He is distributing good Christian literature, and is worthy of sympathy and practical support.

ROBERT HUME, Presbyterian Minister.

Spanish River, August 19, 1898.
From the NORTH STAR, Parry Sound, July 28, 1898.

"Geo. Buskin, of the Colportage Mission of Algoma and the North-West, called by some the Wheelbarrow Evangelist, is in town pursuing the work of the Mission, and is supplying biblical literature, suitable for young or old, and purposes conducting open air gospel services in connection with the work. Many in the town will remember the missionary's first visit here in May, 1876, and the active Christian work then pursued by him. There was then but one religious meeting house—the Methodist—which gave place to the new one now standing, the Episcopalians then using the Temperance Hall. He then conducted prayer and Gospel services in the Court House, School House, Temperance Hall, and the open air, and at Parry Harbor, also in the mill boarding house and in the sample room of the McKee Hotel, and endeavored to have had a Union Hall built there for the same purpose, but failed in the attempt. The object then sought in coming to Parry Sound at that time was to establish a work for Muskoka and the District, something in the form now pursued; and though now much is being done compared with former times, there is much left undone that ought to be attended to. Any who would like to help further the good work will find the Missionary around the town or at Mrs. McCoy's boarding house, and he will also be pleased to supply any who need from his stock of Bibles and biblical literature. The preacher's meetings will be conducted at 7 in the evenings near the post office corner." (Though 20 years have passed since the proposition to build the meeting house for Divine service at Parry Harbor, the only place of the kind as yet built there has been by the Roman Catholics.)

The following names are associate helpers, who will receive and communicate contributions on behalf of. the Mission, all of

which will be duly acknowledged by G. Buskin, Missionary, to the donors :
Toronto—Mrs. S. Vernoy, 231 Jarvis St.
Montreal—G. H. & Robt. Harrower, McGill St.
Ottawa—W. W. Stephen, oil and color merchant.
Hamilton—F. S. Morison, Seneca Jones, J. K. Applegath.
Brantford—Edwin Chalcraft, market square.
London—N. F. Yeo, Dundas St.
Guelph—B. Savage and S. Powel.
Halifax—J. J. Hunt, barrister.
Kingston—John A. Gardiner, 151 Wellington St.
Brockville—Allen Cameron.
Windsor and Walkerville—J. W. Blackadder, box 59, Windsor.
Peterborough—Miss Elizabeth Andrews, 182 Rubridge St.
Galt- R. J. Struthers and A. H. Goodall.
Barrie—Fred. Marr, box 149.
Chatham—A. Hall, box 488.
Sarnia—Robert MacAdam, office *Sarnia Canadian*.
St. Thomas—S. Fraine & Co., tailors.
Port Hope—Joseph Hooper.
Dundas—F. A. Latshaw.
Belleville—A. Ray, druggist.
Clinton—F. W. Watts.
Ingersoll—Dr. F. D. Canfield.
Georgetown—Dr. W. J. Roe.
Paris—F. R. Morgan, grocer.
Strathroy—Mr. Follinsbee, barrister.
St. Marys—H. Whitworth, box 284.
Orangeville—Mrs. Dr. C. M. Smith.
Niagara Falls, Ont—Edward S. Cole, jeweler.
Goderich—Levi Card.
Napanee—F. Arnot, jeweler, box 383.
Detroit, Mich.—Dr. John S. Owen, 23 Adams Ave.

Form of Bequest.

The following short form of bequest has been prepared in the hope that by God's blessing, some who are in possession of temporal substance, which they have found difficult in life to use for Christian work as freely as they would like, may consider the need and privilege for the use of sanctified wealth in the work of God's kingdom. And also, that those who have contributed to help the foregoing mission, may find a pleasure in continuing their aid after their decease, by a bequest, which if embodied in the donor's will, will secure to it valuable and needed aid:

FORM.

I bequeath to the International Evangelical and Scriptural Colportage Mission of Algoma and the North-West, the sum of ....,....................Dollars, to be paid to G. Buskin, Missionary, or in case of his death, to his successor, at the end of three calendar months from my decease; out of such part of my personal estate as the law permits to be bequeathed to charitable purposes.

Christian Home Colonization Association.

AN AGRICULTURAL COLONY FOR THE INDUSTRIOUS POOR.

"The liberal deviseth liberal things; and by liberal things shall he stand."—Isa. 31:8.
Royal Law, "Love thy neighbor as thyself."—Lev. 19:18.
Christ's word, "Love your enemies."—Matt. 5:55.
"What doth it profit, my brethren, to say 'be warmed and filled,' notwithstanding ye give not those things which are needful for the body."—James 2:14-16.

(First printed in BROCKVILLE EVENING RECORDER,
April 7th, 1896.)

A ten acre homestead, or larger if desirable, and a comfortable dwelling permanently and inalienably secured for all time by complying with the necessary conditions of the above Association, is the proposition herein made, to be the result of personal and mutual industry, and a beneficial combination of capital and labor, having good will to each other.

With a multitude of partially employed and destitute persons and families in our large towns and cities, what better plan can be devised than that of filling our unoccupied lands with this surplus population, and thus provide the needy with permanent employment, happy homes and surroundings. This can and ought to be done. To do so calls forth this attempt. To neglect it will end in widespread grief. The world's well-being cannot be maintained by the superabundance of the few, but by the equitable distribution of the earth's supplies among its multitudinous and needy inhabitants.

Investments and endowments for carrying out this proposition, for the time being, can be deposited with Geo. Buskin, of the Algoma Colportage Mission, 202 King street east, Toronto, Ont., until there be properly formulated central and local committees. This is proposed upon the broad principles of Christianity, and not to further denominationalism, whether old or young, or party politics.

The tillage of the land and the raising of cattle is the oldest, happiest, safest, most natural, independent and truly honorable of occupations, and a certain source of wealth. The hasty rush to become rich by other means often ends in disappointment; and if attained by other than honest labor, forethought and production, thereby serving the necessities of others, as well as receiving service from them, is very unsatisfactory to every honest mind.

An architect's plan for comfortable dwellings (see page 175) commencing with a kitchen and ending with a comfortable, roomy and substantial brick house, with all necessary conveniences, has been prepared; cost of kitchen and cellar, $300; building complete as outlined, $600; price made easy by cheap material and labor.

The size of proposed colony, 10 miles square, containing 64,000 acres, obtainable from the Government at about 30c per acre. One thousand men or families could find homes and labor, having a house and 10 or more acres of land for gardening, pasture, etc., and cattle, to be their own in three years, upon payment of capital invested. Fifty-four thousand acres would then be left for the benefit of the capitalists, to be used for dairy and grain; the timber, also could be turned to profit. Each man or family to pay for their own land, buildings, receiving the 10 acres at the Government price, but adding the cost of improvement, to be paid for either at the time of occupation or by instalments, with moderate rates of interest, until paid in full, cottages to be built and paid for in a similar manner. The workmen to occupy 10,000 acres in the centre of the 64,000 acres, which would form the nucleus of a town of a little more than four miles square, from which afterwards allotments could be made and sold for markets, parks and public places.

This work could be started in sections, if not as a whole, and being commenced and conducted with justice, prudence, industry and sincerity, must prove a mutual benefit, drawing off surplus labor, causing increased manufacture and a safe investment for capital. $150,000 would give a start for one-fourth of the colony, and less capital would be required to work the remaining portion. It would not be as much as is required to build some of the present-day religious meeting houses, and would be equally a monument to the praise of God. To be satisfactory, all must be done in order, and the workmen's lot must be drawn for by lot, and be convenient to their work and each other. Their wages should not be less than $1 per day by the year. But idlers, the profane and intemperate should have no place there, but be regarded as criminals. A good and wise man having oversight of 10 men should have something extra.

The workmen in addition to their wages should have a percentage in the profits, with also an opportunity to invest in the capital in any measure they were able so to do. This also would serve to enlarge their interest in the progress of the colony. A week's labour should be limited to 56 or 60 hours, and their wages not to be withheld more than a month—but daily before the sun is down is God's ordinance, Deut. 24:15; James 5:4, and many other passages—and in case any should require to leave their location, they could sell their improvements on the 10 acre lots and the advantage of the time, by any mutual arrangement that could be made.

To start the colony there would be needed horses, cattle, waggons, sleighs, harness, portable steam engines, saw mills and tools of various kinds; and in clearing the woods the timber could be cut and used and sold. Houses, stables and barns would be needed. Government grants could be had for making roads. With judicious management it would be a safe investment for capital, and a means of wealth to the country, making happy homes for multitudes, and in such social life many would be content to live and labor. The men who would practically unite in the enterprise should mutually pledge to hold and abide in the foundation of the Christian faith, acknowledging one God and Father of all, one Lord Jesus Christ, one Holy Spirit the Comforter, the Holy Scripture as God's revelation to man, and maintain the assembling together on the first day of the week, for thanksgiving, praise and prayer to Almighty God, and for the reading and exposition of God's holy word apart from all denominational prejudice, peculiarity of dogmatism, holding to Christ who is the only and the universal head of the universal Christian Church, and His word the only and infallible guide, and to pursue a peaceable and quiet life in all godliness and honesty, it being the sure path of good will and prosperity.

Among the necessities would be a good practical agriculturist from one of the Government Colleges as soon as a sufficient clearing of a thousand acres more or less, had been made and ready for work; also an agricultural school might be established for the settlers, as a business and mercantile appendage.

Some benevolent or wealthy business person may make the necessary investments for some persons or families who could not help themselves, by loaning the necessary money or being security for them, for their 10 acre lot, the buildings and other necessary costs, their investment and interest thereon to be secured from the results of colonists' labours, and premises, time would necessarily be required before proper returns would be made.

Proposed that $100,000 be raised by benevolence, and investments as stockholders, and by debentures, with power to enlarge the amount in a small measure if necessary. That the calls for this amount shall be made in four or five instalments, covering a period of twelve or eighteen months. This amount also to be supplemented by Government and municipal grants; and in return the municipalities might send eligible persons from among their poor to find a home and occupation in the colony. I have estimated, and before enumerated and stated, that about $150,000 directly applied would be sufficient to meet the requirements of 250 locaters and families until there should be a return from their labor, which would be one-fourth of the settlement. The first batch of pioneers, numbering two or three score, must of necessity have capacity for bush and farm work. In working out the balance of lots, the proportion of investment would be greatly reduced. This proposition is not intended in any wise to conflict with the Government's free grant of two hundred acres, to any who have means and energy to carry out the design of the grant; but many attempting the same get discouraged by solitude, circumstances and insufficiency of their means, and their labor is frequently unfruitful. Not so with that herein proposed. Sociability, good order, necessary supplies and Christian character will obviate this difficulty.

Perhaps some mill owner, merchant or wealthy manufacturer may see his way to make an investment in the interest of the colony, to erect, as circumstances may require, saw mill, grist and woollen mill, furniture and manufactures upon principles as before stated, thereby adding success and comfort to the colony, furnishing material for houses and buildings, etc. Such an investment need not interfere in the least with the home manufacturing of each settler in the old country custom of spinning, weaving and manufacturing of small wares for home and export beyond seas and Dominion lines. Here also I will say that a separate and similar colony might also be established to profit for those who have been under the discipline of the law. Many of them who, leaving the place of seclusion, know not which way to turn for the best, and to them also might be shown the Samaritan's good will, by our love to our enemies.

I am thankful to say the project has been approved by some of our able friends, including one of our active M.P.P.'s and others, and especially one—for whose good will to our Christian endeavor in years past we still esteem ourselves a debtor—taking time to consider the subject, giving valuable counsel; also giving a word of introduction and commendation to the Commissioner of Crown Lands, who promised at some later time, after receiving an explicit statement, to give the necessary attention and reply to it.

There are three localities which might be selected, each may have their own advantages and disadvantages for the colony: one is the Spanish and French river neighborhood, the other the Temiscamingue and the Rainy River district. Time and means will be required to make a suitable choice. The Spanish or French river district would be the nearest to commence if a suitable area can be found there; the others might also be worked in a similar form at a later period. In concluding this brief proposition, I must add: Having named it a Christian Colonization Association, it includes the business traits that are honorable and profitable. The wide world is open as a market for all that energy, thought, and good will can devise and produce. Crowning it all, to do well there must be, Glory to God in the highest. This principle actuates every true Christian; therefore let all its business be begun, pursued and ended by thanksgiving, praise and supplication to Him. He has said: "I will be glorified," and that for all the good He has promised His people He will be enquired of to do it for them.

The 10 acre proposition is an old institution. The division

of the land of Canaan by Moses gave to each family about ten acres of land, and the mortgagee could not hold it beyond the jubilee or 50th year, but it would have to return to its original owners. Their whole history shows that abundance of sheep and cattle was largely the source of their wealth. The same allotments have been found to work profitably in the lands of Europe and Great Britain. See Encyclopædia Brittanica, under the heads of land tenure, holdings, communism, socialism, farm and forestry, therein dealt with, in the light of Divine and human law and wisdom, apart from the extravagant excesses and reckless contentions, and it gives the evidences of the successful working of small allotments of land.

Some have asked, "What can be done on ten acres of land?" This is a question asked by many who do not understand the design of the proposed 10 acre Christian homestead colony and dwellings for the industrious poor, the ultimate view of which is the tillage and pasturage of more than 50,000 acres in a block, which would be additional, affording constant employment as well as homes for more than a thousand families. Each ten acres properly cultivated would abundantly supply for each family their necessities, and leave a surplus for export of grain, cattle, hogs, butter, cheese, wool, etc.; and many other advantages would result from the application of labor upon the wild and unoccupied lands, and the establishment there of the industrious poor in permanent homesteads and dwellings of their own. The yield of ten acres with ordinary labor and judgment would be: From one acre sufficient vegetables for family use, viz., 20 bags of potatoes, 1,000 cabbages, 2 tons of turnips, 10 bushels of onions, 2,000 heads of celery, and 30 rods or near ¼ acre for beans, peas, beets, radishes, etc.; 4 acres for pasture and hay to maintain 2 cows to produce milk and butter for family use, and to make 10 lbs. of butter per week for 7 months; 2 acres sown in wheat will yield 40 bushels of wheat which will give 1,700 lbs. of flour to feed family, and 600 lbs. of shorts to feed stock; 1 acre sown in carrots and turnips for feed and sale will give 10 tons of carrots and 15 tons of turnips; 1 acre of potatoes will yield 150 bags; 1 acre of peas from 20 to 25 bushels, which with small potatoes will fat 800 lbs. of pork, 300 lbs. for family use and 500 lbs. for sale; can also feed 25 fowls for eggs for family use, keep 2 ewe sheep, 1 brood sow for stock. All straw to go for feed. This would yield $180 cash beyond keeping the family, viz: butter, $28; carrots, $50; turnips, $40; potatoes $27; pork, $25. Three horses would do all necessary work on 10 lots or 100 acres, and this can be multiplied 1,000 or 10,000 fold. Thus the proper cultivation of the 54,000 additional acres would be constant employment for the 1,000 families, and humanly speaking, be a certain source of comfort and wealth by the application of ordinary labor and proper judgment.

How many now in this time of opportunity and need would venture five thousand dollars each, less or more, to enrich the poor and themselves in the formation of the proposed 10 acre Christian homestead colony and dwellings for the industrious poor, giving them 10 years to repay investments on their behalf, and furnishing them with work upon the 50,000 acre farm, whereby they could repay all investments?

A selection from a letter in the "Hamilton Spectator," Feb. 4, 1897: "Among all the schemes for helping the poor and unemployed, there are none that have the elements of permanent help, and how preposterous it seems, that when we have the means at hand, to be doling out our charity year after year, and the condition of the recipients getting worse and worse. With all our vacant land, and our anxiousness for emigrants, why not with some of this money get the most of these people on a piece, say 10 or 20 acres, according to the quality of the land, then pay instructors to teach those who are ignorant, for one year; when all such would be permanently established, where by their own labor they would be able to make a comfortable living and raise their children where they were intended to be raised, on God's acres—and not on street corners. In the cities the wife and families are comparatively helpless, while on the land each can help to make a living, and are away from mischief. I hope Mr. Buskin will unfold a feasible plan."—Mrs. McGee Smith. This is one of the many enquiries resulting from the proposition of the ten acre colony which means to say, go on and success attend you. Who is willing to lead the way and invest sums, either large or small, and set the work in motion? In answer to an application made on its behalf to the Commissioner of the Crown Lands department enquiring for suitable location, and what assistance the Government might be disposed to give to help it, a reply dated March 10th, 1897, concludes by saying, "Perhaps you will let it rest till after the session, when it will be taken up and fully considered." No answer yet received.

Some competent persons who have considered the matter, and whose minds have been previously exercised concerning the need of practical assistance for the poor, who are unable to help themselves, have suggested that the Government should take it up, and make it constitutional and workable for the whole Dominion, and doubtless, before long, a committee will in some way be formed to transform the theory into a workable and working matter-of-fact reality.

Those who can approve of this proposed work, are respectfully reminded that if among their acquaintances any are benevolently disposed, the favor of their commendation is desired; but if personally they have the power to forward a donation, or investment, upon interest at 3 per cent. per annum for a period of 5 or 10 years, please lead the way, and then your friends or neighbors will be more disposed to do the same. It is Godlike to give to the poor, for God has given us all things, and His Son Jesus to die for our sins, and without His goodness and mercy where would any of us be? Should you not have sufficient cash on hand for the investment you may be willing to make, send what proportion of the amount you are able, and a promissory note for the balance upon which current rate of interest would have to be paid to be of service. A printed form can be sent to intending investors upon receipt of their first donation or investment.

Intending colonists can also make investments in the same manner and at the same rate of interest until their money shall be applied upon the land and improvements and stock on their behalf.

www.ingramcontent.com/pod-product-compliance
Lightning Source LLC
Chambersburg PA
CBHW020842160426
43192CB00007B/746